DESIGN + ENVIRONMENT
A GLOBAL GUIDE TO DESIGNING GREENER GOODS

Helen Lewis and John Gertsakis
with Tim Grant, Nicola Morelli and Andrew Sweatman

HELEN LEWIS is Programme Manager, Sustainable Products and Product Systems, for the Centre for Design at RMIT in Melbourne, Australia. She has worked as a Programme Manager on the EcoReDesign™ programme at RMIT, and is a co-author of *Good Design, Better Business, Cleaner World: A Guide to EcoReDesign™* (Centre for Design at RMIT University, 1997). Prior to this she was Manager Industry Programmes at EcoRecycle Victoria, a state government agency with responsibility for waste minimisation and resource recovery. At EcoRecycle, she managed grant programmes to assist manufacturers with new product development and marketing, and co-ordinated strategies to increase recovery of recyclable materials.

helen.lewis@rmit.edu.au

JOHN GERTSAKIS is the Managing Director of Product Ecology Pty Ltd, a sustainability consulting group experienced in the development and delivery of tools, strategies and advice on EcoDesign and Product Stewardship. John has written widely on a range of issues related to the design, production and consumption of environmentally preferable products, including the Centre for Design's *EcoReDesign™ Guide*. He sits on the editorial board of *The International Journal for Sustainable Product Design*, and has authored, co-authored and edited several handbooks, reports and websites including: 'Connecting Innovation, Design and Sustainability: Real World Case Studies from the EcoReDesign™ Program' (2001); 'Appliance Reuse and Recycling: A Product Stewardship Guide' (1999); 'EcoSpecifier: A Guide to Sourcing Environmentally Preferable Materials' (1999); and 'Good Design, Better Business, Cleaner World: A Guide to EcoReDesign™' (1997). Prior to Product Ecology, John was Head of the Centre for Design at RMIT University (1997–2001), where he continues to be involved as a Senior Research Associate.

john@productecology.com.au

TIM GRANT is the project manager for life-cycle assessment at the Centre for Design at RMIT University. He has experience applying LCA and other environmental tools with a wide range of companies and organisations. He has developed and refined a number of LCA tools specifically for use in ecodesign, as well as being involved in the development and application of LCA data and methodology in Australia. Tim also runs a professional development short course in LCA at the Centre for Design.

tim.grant@rmit.edu.au

NICOLA MORELLI is a graduate in architecture from Italy and has a PhD in industrial design at Politecnico di Milano. Currently, Nicola Morelli is a post-doctoral researcher at RMIT University in Melbourne. His research work is focused on sustainable design strategies, based on systemic changes in production and consumption patterns.

nicola.morelli@rmit.edu.au

ANDREW SWEATMAN is an environmental consultant and Director of Customer Applications with ESHconnect in California, USA. Andrew has formal qualifications in product design and has been involved as a researcher and project manager with RMIT's EcoReDesign™ programme as well as Manchester Metropolitan University's Design for Environment research project. At ESHconnect, Andrew is managing the development of innovative online regulatory tracking tools related to electronics and the environment and works closely with leading product manufacturers in the USA.

asweatman@yahoo.com

design + environment

a global guide to designing greener goods

HELEN LEWIS and JOHN GERTSAKIS
with TIM GRANT, NICOLA MORELLI and ANDREW SWEATMAN

Greenleaf
PUBLISHING
2001

© 2001 Greenleaf Publishing Limited

Published by Greenleaf Publishing Limited
Aizlewood's Mill
Nursery Street
Sheffield S3 8GG
UK

The paper used for this book is made from wood grown in well managed
and sustainable forests
Printed in Great Britain by Chris Fowler International Ltd, London.
Cover design by Lali Abril.

British Library Cataloguing in Publication Data:
   Lewis, Helen
     Design + environment : a global guide to designing greener
     goods
     1. New products 2. Green products - Design
     I. Title II. Gertsakis, John
     658.5 ' 752

     ISBN 1874719438

Mixed Sources
Product group from well-managed
forests and other controlled sources
www.fsc.org Cert no. TT-COC-2191
© 1996 Forest Stewardship Council

CONTENTS

FOREWORD

Graham Cavanagh-Downs
**Director, Manufacturing and Supply,
Fuji Xerox Australia**

In the past, 'green programmes' were seen by many as 'soft', 'reactive' and 'feel-good'. However, more and more companies have realised that environmental management is a key strategic business issue with the potential for a lasting impact on company performance.

In the future all companies will need to implement strategies to reduce the environmental impacts of their products and services. For some, environmental management is seen as a necessary evil, with little economic benefit. This is a very short-sighted view. In fact, companies failing to address environmental performance in product design and development will find it increasingly difficult to be competitive in the coming century.

Environmental factors must be viewed as a stimulus for innovation and more efficient allocation of business resources, not just as an issue of regulatory compliance. Success in addressing these factors provides exciting new terrain for competition, and new ways to add value to core business programmes.

Life-cycle assessment at the product development stage provides benefits to the environment and the bottom line. By adopting a life-cycle approach, companies will uncover opportunities for waste reduction, re-use of resources and the development of recycling and remanufacturing programmes.

An opportunity now exists for companies to take a holistic approach to environmental performance that includes design for the environment and product stewardship programmes such as product take-back initiatives.

What is good for the environment is good for business. *Design + Environment* provides practical guidelines, tools and case studies to help companies meet the challenge of improving environmental performance while developing business strategies to secure long-term growth.

ACKNOWLEDGEMENTS

This book is the result of many ideas and many experiences. It is also the outcome of collaboration and information exchange over several years. While the book's origins can be traced to the Centre for Design at the Royal Melbourne Institute of Technology (RMIT)'s EcoReDesign™ programme, the content also reflects knowledge and experience gained by the authors through other programmes, both within RMIT and beyond. It reflects the diversity, evolution, challenges and opportunities associated with the development of ecodesign over an eight-year period.

The authors would like to acknowledge the contribution of other people who have been involved in the EcoReDesign™ programme at RMIT and who have therefore contributed, directly or indirectly, to the material in this book. Professor Chris Ryan was instrumental in establishing the programme and was one of the co-authors of the *Guide to EcoReDesign™*. The contribution of other staff members, past and present, including Michael Abdilla, Kate Lumb and Henry Okraglik, is also gratefully acknowledged. Alan Pears, Professor Douglas Tomkin, Deni Greene, Gerry Mussett and Mark Armstrong acted as consultants to the programme and were valued members of the team.

PREFACE

The aim of this book is to provide practical information for designers interested in minimising the environmental impacts of products.

The book is designed as a workbook rather than as an academic text. It should be read once, and then used as a reference or workbook.

Chapter 1 includes some background information to help you understand how and why design for environment (DfE) has become so critical to design, with reference to some of the most influential writers, designers and companies in the field. International trends that are driving environmental design are discussed, including a shift to more regulatory approaches to the environmental management of products, particularly in northern Europe countries, Japan and the USA. The increasing regulation of products has provided an opportunity for innovative companies to take the initiative in designing new and improved products. Some of these companies have become market leaders in a highly competitive market.

Chapter 2 provides a step-by-step approach to DfE. The principles are not difficult or complex—they simply add another dimension to the design brief. The aim of DfE is to design a product that meets requirements for quality, cost, manufacturability and consumer appeal, while at the same time minimising environmental impacts. The first step in the process is to undertake an assessment of environmental impacts, by using life-cycle assessment (LCA) or one of the many simpler tools available to help the designer. An LCA identifies some of the issues to be addressed in the design brief. From then on, DfE becomes an integral part of the normal design process, including the development of concepts, design of prototypes, final design and development of marketing strategies.

Environmental assessment tools are discussed in Chapter 3. These range from simple qualitative methods to more complex, quantitative tools.

Strategies to reduce environmental impacts are presented in more detail in Chapter 4. The designer needs to select appropriate strategies at a very early stage in the design process. For example, which materials have least impact on the environment? Are any of the traditional materials hazardous? Are there alternative materials? Energy and water efficiency must also be considered in the design of any electrical or electronic product. In many cases the selection of strategies must consider trade-offs: for example, the impact of lightweight materials on recyclability.

Chapter 5 highlights some of the links between environmental problems and the everyday products we consume. In order to design products with minimal environmental impact, we need to have a basic understanding of these impacts and the interactions between them. They include issues such as global warming, ozone depletion, and water and air pollution.

Chapters 6–9 include more detailed strategies and case studies for particular product groups, including packaging (Chapter 6), textiles and clothing (Chapter 7), furniture (Chapter 8), and electrical and electronic products (Chapter 9). Guidelines are provided for each of the critical stages of a product's life, from the selection of raw materials through to strategies for recovery and recycling.

Chapter 10 takes a look at some of the emerging trends in DfE that are offering us the opportunity to make a more significant reduction in environmental impacts. New and more sustainable materials and technologies are being developed. Companies are also starting to reconsider their relationship to the market by offering to lease rather than sell products to consumers. This provides them with a range of options, such as the opportunity to upgrade features rather than develop a new and 'better' model. It also enables them to recover old products for repair, remanufacturing or recovery of materials.

Our involvement in RMIT's EcoReDesign™ programme has highlighted the scarcity of good, practical resources for designers interested in this area and led to the writing of this book. Parts of the book are based on material developed earlier for *A Guide to EcoReDesign™*, but most of the material is new.

1

INTRODUCTION

1.1 Overview

International trends are demonstrating that concepts and tools such as design for environment (DfE), life-cycle assessment (LCA) and extended producer responsibility (EPR) are here to stay. They are rapidly becoming key tools for forward-thinking corporations. Furthermore, a growing body of evidence suggests that such approaches are exceptionally well placed to deliver a range of benefits over and above environmental benefits and mere compliance. These 'new millennium' tools will revolutionise how business creates new products and services and how consumers and government will compare, assess, regulate and purchase every-day goods.

In particular, DfE provides a unique opportunity to make critical interventions early in the product development process and eliminate, avoid or reduce downstream environmental impacts. What will emerge as a continuing thread throughout this book is that DfE is a technical and creative 'key'—a device that can substantially determine how a product is likely to interact with the environment and its users. In other words, DfE can make considerable environmental and commercial gains based on the basic philosophy that 'prevention is better than cure'.

1.1.1 Environmental improvement: why focus on design?

Environmental impacts occur at all stages of a product's life-cycle. Different types of products have impacts at different stages of the life-cycle. For example, for furniture the raw materials and final disposal embody most of the environmental impacts, and for energy-consuming products such as household appliances the use of the product embodies most of the environmental impact. However, no matter where in the product life-cycle the impact lies, most of the impact is 'locked' into the product at the design stage when materials are selected and product performance is largely determined. This concept is represented in Figure 1.1, along with the types of strategy used to address environmental performance along a product development cycle.

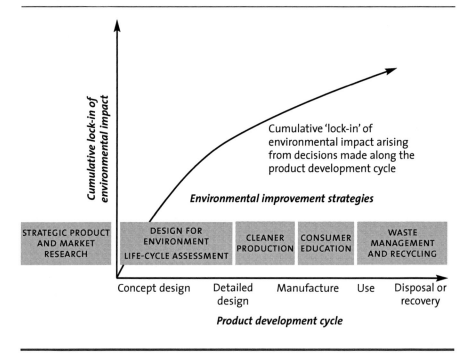

Figure 1.1 **Conceptual representation of environmental 'lock-in' over a product's development cycle**

At a very practical level, DfE, accompanied by a judicious use of LCA, provides one of the most powerful tools in pursuit of sustainable products. It is at the product planning and design stage that waste avoidance, source reduction, water conservation and energy efficiency can be locked into products, services and buildings. Trying to implement such strategies once the design is resolved or settled generally reflects an 'end-of-pipe' orientation and represents 'yesterday's thinking'.

What becomes apparent—whether one is considering a domestic appliance, food packaging, office furniture or textiles—is that only a life-cycle design approach can lock in positive environmental features and lock out undesirable environmental impacts. At a policy level, it is a genuine product stewardship approach that embodies the principles of EPR, with brand-owners taking much greater responsibility for their products when they are discarded.

The overarching significance of DfE is further reinforced by the expanding list of companies allocating substantial resources to sustainable product development. Their creation of environmentally improved products is not only testament to serious corporate environmental foresight but also an acute reminder that the sceptics have got it wrong. Regardless of the goods produced, DfE is becoming a key strategy motivating many of today's companies, including Philips Electronics, Hewlett-Packard, Interface, Wilkhahn, Herman Miller, Miele, Electrolux, Xerox, BMW and Daimler-Benz—to name but a few.

On the subject of companies, methods and sustainability in isolation of people can only go so far. Good design, sustainable design, commercially successful design requires smart thinkers, enthusiastic individuals, committed teams and progressive executives (i.e. innovative eco-product developers).

1.2 Critical players:
the role of designers and product developers

It becomes vividly apparent that those professions and trades involved in designing new products are key players in helping realise a more sustainable future. Whether it is the formally trained industrial designer, engineer, model-maker, marketing manager, psychologist, technical writer, toolmaker or plastics specialist—we need to recognise that many areas of knowledge work together and toward the development of environmentally preferable products. In many ways it is more accurate to talk about eco-product developers rather than of ecodesigners.

Working alone, the designer's environmental role is limited; in combination with other disciplines, the designer emerges as a critical player in ensuring that a diverse and sometimes conflicting range of issues and considerations are successfully built into a product. It is ultimately the designer who creates the interface between the consumer and the technology underlying the shell or surface of a manufactured product. Thus the designer's ability to play the role of environmental champion is unequalled compared with others.

An interdisciplinary approach is not only an essential requirement of successful DfE but also a highly desirable approach if we want to maximise the commercial and environmental performance of a manufactured product. Collaboration facilitated by a genuine enthusiasm to learn, share, evolve, explore, innovate, discover and apply environmental qualities is likely to result in the rethinking and reconfiguring of the product development process on all fronts, not just the environmental front.

We simply need to look around us, wherever we are, and note the almost infinite extent to which designers shape our physical and virtual worlds. It is ultimately the designer who gives form and meaning to objects that not only offer utility, function and convenience but also entertainment, desire and visual pleasure. However, although a growing number of designers are openly acknowledging that they wish to be part of the solution that is sustainable development, many designers and others involved in product development seem to feel paralysed or restrained from having a positive or significant environmental effect on the design process.

Recognising that the designer or the product development team can take practical action to shape, fashion and model ideas and concepts into sustainable products, it must also be acknowledged that the goal is not to transform designers into environmental scientists. It is about blending environmental considerations into the roles of all in the product development team—be they designers, engineers, psychologists, marketers, toolmakers or executives. Above all, designers and product developers need to throw off their shackles and forge ahead on implementing DfE. They must start small, make no-risk or low-risk decisions, establish 'environmental' dialogue with suppliers and other stakeholders and, most of all, remember there are probably many common-sense design decisions that they have already been making that equate with DfE. Although some academics emphasise complex methodologies that may blur and burden DfE, the reality is that many significant environmental improvements can be realised through the use of basic checklists and general rules of thumb.

In other words, you do not need to be a rocket scientist to successfully implement DfE strategies within a commercial context. Understanding the jargon and terminology may help, though.

1.3 What's in a name? Some definitions

Accurate descriptors or buzzwords? What is design for environment and where does it sit on the spectrum of other terms related to environmentally oriented product design? Is it different from green design, ecodesign and sustainable design?

The answer to these questions depends on who you ask; however, the ultimate goal or end-point associated with such terms remains similar: that is, designing products as though the environment matters, and minimising their direct and indirect environmental impacts at every possible opportunity.

In essence, whether the process is referred to as DfE or ecodesign, the fundamental objective is to design products with the environment in mind and to assume some responsibility for the product's environmental consequences as they relate to specific decisions and actions executed during the design process. Obviously, the designer cannot bear responsibility for all negative effects; however, the designer *can* have a significant influence over the environmental impacts that may arise upstream and downstream of his or her own interaction.

A robust DfE approach is one that blends creative excellence, innovation and technical rigour with a view to fearlessly pursuing major environmental and functional objectives. Ultimately, products have a function and a purpose, and this must remain the designer's priority. The challenge is to assert product functionality while simultaneously minimising life-cycle environmental impacts and maximising competitiveness.

One of the critical adjuncts to DfE over the past decade has been incorporation of LCA, sometimes more popularly referred to as cradle-to-grave analysis. LCA is one of the most useful tools in identifying and assessing the environmental aspects and potential impacts associated with a product. The value of LCA is in its ability to map a product's environmental impact across its whole life-cycle, including:

- Extraction and processing of raw materials

- Manufacture of the product (and any associated packaging and consumables)

- Use or operation of product

- End-of-life options (e.g. re-use, remanufacture, recycling, treatment and disposal)

A critical distribution or transport phase usually occurs between all the above stages and can have a significant impact on a product's life-cycle environmental impacts.

It is this life-cycle perspective that has formed the cornerstone of DfE and won the support and acknowledgement of progressive governments and corporations, of the global environment movement and of an ever-growing list of influential designers. In design terms, LCA can perform practical functions as well as more strategic tasks.

Use of LCA as a DfE tool can:

- Benchmark the environmental performance of existing products

- Develop environmental targets for the product development team to pursue

- Provide a 'work-in-progress' assessment tool to review how a concept or detailed design might perform environmentally

- Help the product development team make decisions regarding materials and components

- Identify previously unknown impacts associated with a product and associated consumables

The collective outcome of using LCA to provide the above data can inform and direct the design process like no other environmental management tool. Despite its practical value and unique product profiling qualities, LCA does have its limitations and constraints. Poor quality of input data, questionable assumptions, sloppy methodologies and debatable interpretation can all undermine or 'contaminate' LCA. However, when ethically and rigorously utilised, it can significantly enhance the potency of DfE. For more detail on specific LCA strategies and tools, see Chapter 3.

When defined and applied strictly, approaches such as sustainable design or sustainable product development begin to deviate from the way most designers perceive and apply DfE. Sustainable design begins to address the bigger picture by considering collectively some of the harder questions, such as need, equity, ethics, social impact and total resource efficiency and thus the role of design in achieving inter-generational equity. More specifically, sustainable design seeks to translate and embody global and regional socio-environmental concerns into products and services at the local level. This necessarily demands a systems view of design and does not always focus on realising physical products.

Buzzwords often associated with sustainable design include dematerialisation, product-to-service strategies, 'Factor 4' and 'Factor 20' goals as well as backcasting and other modelling tools (see also Box 1.1). The aim is to minimise incremental 'tinkering' through end-of-pipe environmental management, cleaner production and DfE, and to maximise robust system-wide solutions in pursuit of more sustainable modes of production and consumption. This is discussed further in Chapter 10.

When a designer is immersed in the design process, trying to meet a client's expectations and to satisfy consumer desires, terminology can become peripheral. What is obvious and central to the task is that DfE is an approach concerned with delivering meaningful environmental benefits, possible only through mainstreaming environmental concerns and realising low-impact products that are culturally relevant, economically viable, technically innovative and ecologically compatible.

THE FOLLOWING IS A PALETTE OF TERMS THAT IN SOME WAY DEFINE OR REFER TO environmentally sensitive product design.

- Design for environment
- Ecological design
- Environmental design
- Environmentally oriented design
- Ecologically oriented design
- Environmentally responsible design
- Socially responsible design
- Sustainable product design
- Sustainable product development
- Green design
- Life-cycle design
- Dematerialisation
- Eco-efficiency
- Biodesign

No doubt the list will grow as the area develops.

Box 1.1 **A palette of buzzwords**

1.4 Origins and evolution: an historical snapshot

The origins of DfE as we understand it today probably lie somewhere between the incisive critique of Victor Papanek and the maturing attitudes and actions of industry. Few would argue against Papanek's watershed contribution to the debate surrounding designers and their obligations to society and the environment. Although other writers argued the case against rampant consumerism, maverick manufacturers, poor architecture and life-threatening products (see e.g. Buckminster Fuller, cited in Pawley 1990; Nader 1965; Neutra 1954; Packard 1956), it was Papanek who focused the ethical blowtorch on the industrial design profession.

Papanek's landmark text—*Design for the Real World: Human Ecology and Social Change* (1971)—was one of the more critical contributions towards raising the profile of designers' less successful projects and behaviour. His critique of the design professions, their clients in industry and the associated educational institutions was scathing but accurate. The core of his argument was that designers focused far too much effort on the aesthetic and stylistic aspects of design rather than considering the whole product—its function, utility, reparability, affordability and its environmental and social consequences.

Papanek's sequel—*The Green Imperative: Ecology and Ethics in Design and Architecture* (1995)—was in many respects an updating of *Design for the Real World*, with an emphasis on the ecological rather than the social aspects.[1] He also reported on the progress of industry and designers by presenting case studies on how DfE has been embodied in products and buildings in more recent years.

Nigel Whitely, in his book *Design for Society* (1993), has continued the Papanek tradition of questioning and critiquing the role of designers in an increasingly consumerist society.[2] Not unlike Papanek in his sequel, Whitely seeks to highlight how design can play a more humane and socially relevant role in meeting the needs of everyday living, be it in the first or the third world.

The problem with both texts is their righteous approach to determining what constitutes good design, bad design, green design and so on. Indeed, some of their propositions, arguments, observations and conclusions are not only religious in their zeal but also consistently fail to account for the extent of DfE activity currently under way in industry, facilitated by governments and acted on by designers.

---

1   Victor Papanek, one of the most eminent working and teaching designers of our time, believes passionately in the power of design to influence our lives and the environment for good or ill. In this inspiring yet practical book he shows how everyone—from those at the forefront of design to the consumers, the end-users, can contribute to the wellbeing of people and planet through a new awareness of design and technology.

2   This is an anti-consumerist-design book in that it exposes what most people would agree are the socially and ecologically unsound values on which consumerist design is constructed. Whitely reviews the implications of ecodesign as part of the movement for a more self-aware and just development of design.

Some of the most exciting developments in recent years have been the emergence of non-conforming designer-based groups that have been proactive in raising the profile of DfE in more general terms. Movements such as O2 continue to expand their programmes of advocacy, promotions, events and lectures. Danish designer Nils Peter Flint gave birth to O2 Denmark, but the O2 Global Network now covers numerous countries around the world. The most refreshing aspect of the O2 groups is its positive and constructive orientation towards DfE. This is further enhanced by the different focus of each group. Whereas some are geared towards running lectures, conferences and publishing newsletters, others operate on a more commercial consulting basis. The O2 Global Network website is definitely worth visiting, at www.O2.org.

As with any special-interest groups, some survive, others perform a function and disappear and yet others expire owing to lack of commitment. The same can be said for DfE-related groups.

Universities and government-funded research institutions have also been pivotal in developing DfE tools, methods and resources. Often located within schools and faculties of engineering and industrial design, the academic research community has made and continues to make a significant contribution towards the evolution and adoption of DfE.

Many of the pioneering universities and research institutions that have forged the DfE path are European and reflect a very strong commitment to environmental protection, investment in research and development (R&D) and a robust design literacy. In particular, the Technical Universities of Delft (TU Delft), Denmark and Berlin[3] have well-established reputations in DfE and in associated areas such as LCA and cleaner production, not to mention strong industrial design engineering programmes. In addition to the TU Delft, another Dutch research organisation— Netherlands Organisation for Applied Scientific Research (TNO)—has been at the epicentre of European and indeed global DfE activity. Together, these two organisations have been, and continue to be, in the vanguard of environmentally oriented product design, successfully executing national demonstration projects such as EcoDesign 1, 2 and 3, including *EcoDesign: A Promising Approach to Sustainable Production and Consumption*, published by the United Nations Environment Programme (UNEP), TU Delft and the Rathenau Institute.

British activity continues to expand through the proactive and dynamic efforts of the Centre for Sustainable Design, based at the Surrey Institute of Art and Design. Numerous other universities across the United Kingdom are focusing on a diverse range of DfE topics and themes. These include Cranfield, Surrey, Brunel and Manchester Metropolitan Universities, all of which are developing new DfE tools that address the needs of key industry sectors, such as electronics, appliances, packaging and commercial furniture.

In Australia, the National Centre for Design at the Royal Melbourne Institute of Technology (RMIT) has conducted some ground-breaking work with manufac-

---

3   Technische Hogeschool te Delft, Delft, the Netherlands; Danmarks Tekniske Højskole, Copenhagen, Denmark; Technische Universität Berlin, Berlin, Germany.

turing companies through its ongoing national demonstration programme—EcoReDesign™. Whereas RMIT has established a strong reputation for hands-on, commercially relevant DfE processes, Sydney's EcoDesign Foundation has carved out a small niche in New South Wales by undertaking more theoretical explorations, primarily in the architectural area.

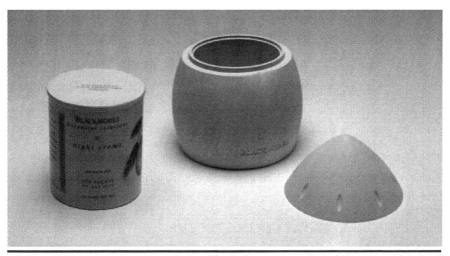

Plate 1.1 **This eco-packaging concept, designed for Blackmores, Australia, includes a re-usable tub and a lightweight refill pack. It was developed through the EcoReDesign™ programme.**

Photo courtesy Centre for Design at RMIT

The extent of activity in the USA is substantial, but not so tightly focused on universities. Although there are several active and productive research institutions, many innovative DfE initiatives have their origins directly in industry. Mindful of export markets, greener institutional customers and growing pressure from the environment movement and other consumer-oriented non-governmental organisations (NGOs), several US-based corporations have played a key role in advancing DfE. By moving beyond concepts and prototypes in some key product categories, US manufacturers have realised some significant gains. Their ability to deliver intense and strong environmental marketing messages has been even more significant. In the electronic office equipment area, companies such as Xerox, Hewlett-Packard, AT&T and IBM have developed a global reputation for attention to DfE, remanufacturing and product stewardship. High-profile office-furniture manufacturers such as Herman Miller, Steelcase and Knoll have also been long-term players in the research, design, manufacture and remanufacture of ergonomic seating, partitions and workstations. Other US corporations with more diverse activities, such as 3M, have and continue to set new and innovative standards when it comes to DfE and positive environmental qualities in products. The Rocky Mountain Institute (Billings, MT) has also promoted innovative research and policy initiatives, particularly in the field of energy conservation.

The overall rate of DfE development has been very much accelerated as a result of the projects and programmes of DfE commentators, nonconformist design groups and universities. However, one of the main drivers behind more serious attention to DfE has been national governments (especially those in northern and western Europe)—there is nothing like the threat of regulation to get industry rethinking its approach to business!

1.5 Big sticks and carrots: the role of government regulation

It is difficult to talk about DfE without noting the significant (and positive) influence that has been exerted by some governments, especially in the Netherlands, Germany and Scandinavia. These countries have been vital in helping facilitate more intense and productive DfE activity in industry. The Dutch and German governments, in particular, have navigated new territory when it comes to the use of new methods and tools to underpin government policy and regulations aimed at improving the environmental performance of industry and its products.

The existence or threat of environmental regulation has had, and continues to have, a considerable influence over some of the larger companies operating in Europe. The regulatory push emanating from Europe is also having a demonstrable effect on product design in the USA, as companies eager to export to Europe and compete with European businesses build in DfE features.

Whether it is aimed at minimising greenhouse gas emissions, increasing energy and water efficiency, developing renewable energy, waste avoidance, resource recovery or eco-labelling, the role of public policy should not be underestimated. Without government intervention, or the threat thereof, it is unlikely that DfE would have come as far as it has. But some governments have been sensitive to provide a careful mix of rewards and incentives as well as stringent environmental laws and targets. The Dutch government, through its Ecodesign initiatives, has mastered the art of demonstration programmes, partly as a way of helping industry prepare for the inevitable tightening of environmental regulations. This balance generates a productive tension between government and business, the government being seen to both regulate and support business.

1.5.1 *Demonstration programmes*

Demonstrating how the design process can integrate environmental factors within a commercial context is a critical step towards reconfiguring the psyche of product designers, engineers, companies, educators and students. It can also directly articulate that DfE does not have to result in inferior, odd or undesirable products plagued by clichéd colours, textures and forms.

Internationally, the demonstration, or 'do, show and tell', approach to DfE has helped to shorten and steepen the learning curve for designers and the companies who rely on them. With support from governments, research institutions and industry associations, countries such as the Netherlands, Norway, Denmark and the United Kingdom have aimed to encourage greater enthusiasm and on-the-ground action ahead of the policy and regulatory change that would otherwise leave industry floundering in search of innovative solutions to serious environmental concerns.

The essential objective of these demonstration programmes is to assist individual companies with the know-how required to design greener products with reduced life-cycle environmental impacts. Ensuring that the products move beyond slick renderings and glossy models is paramount, as is the need to blend a stronger design and environmental philosophy into company culture, especially that of senior management. Documenting the entire process and generating information materials for dissemination to the broader design community directly fulfils the demonstration objective. 'How to' manuals, design guides, videos and computer software collectively provide first-hand knowledge, methods and guidelines based on specific product case studies and real-life commercial experiences.

1.5.2 *Defining extended producer responsibility*

By far one of the most influential areas of government environment policy has been the development and gradual implementation of extended producer responsibility (EPR). In a great number of countries, manufacturers face a very different regulatory environment to that (currently) existing in Australia. As levels of concern over issues of pollution and waste disposal have risen, governments have been forced to act to improve the effectiveness of environmental controls and standards. Government action is most obvious and most 'advanced' in Europe, although many of the European approaches have some counterpart in the USA, Canada, Japan, Korea and Taiwan (for a recent overview of the situation in Japan Korea and Taiwan, see Kuraska 1995: 95-109). In these countries, as a response to government action, there is a clear change in orientation on the part of industry. Strategic planning by leading companies, investment in new technology and production processes, the reorientation of business practice and R&D spending all suggest a broad level of acceptance that issues of waste and pollution are of such significance that major structural change to current industrial production is inevitable.

Environmental regulations cover a range of targets and address a number of issues. Some are focused on eliminating harmful substances or practices: restricting the levels of emission of pollutants; banning the use of certain materials (such as ozone-depleting substances); protecting sensitive environments or habitats; prohibiting the transport of toxic substances; and so on. Other regulations aim at altering the economic or social framework so that harmful activities are discouraged while better practice—or improved practice—is encouraged.

EPR and product stewardship are two names for a principle increasingly being adopted around the world as a basis for government policy and programmes to reduce waste and environmental impacts from the end-of-life disposal of goods. The Organisation for Economic Co-operation and Development (OECD 1997) defines EPR as:

> The principle that manufacturers and importers of products should bear a significant degree of responsibility for the environmental impacts of their products throughout the product life-cycle, including impacts [from] . . . the selection of materials, the . . . production process, and . . . from the use and disposal of the products.

In OECD (1996) terms, the objective of EPR is to 'promote the conservation of resources, reduce the use and generation of toxic and hazardous materials and energy, and reduce the quantity of wastes for final disposal'.

EPR is a logical extension of the 'polluter-pays' principle. It rests on an argument that the environmental impacts of resource depletion, waste and pollution are a function of the system of production and consumption of goods and services. Those impacts are substantially determined at the point of production, which is when key choices are made—on materials, on processing and finishing technology, on product function and durability, on systems of distribution and marketing and so on. If that system is to evolve in a way that reduces environmental impacts, then there is a need for policies that create appropriate feedback mechanisms for producers that will direct producers' investment towards continuous environmental improvement. In many OECD and other countries EPR is considered an effective policy mechanism to promote the integration of the life-cycle environmental costs associated with products into the market price for the product.

Stimulating industry to accept responsibility for its products at the end of their life is an important focus for environmental and industrial policy in Austria, Belgium, Denmark, Finland, France, Germany, Greece, Ireland, Italy, Luxembourg, the Netherlands, Norway, Sweden, Switzerland and the United Kingdom.[4] It also applies in Japan, Taiwan, Canada and in some US states.

1.5.3 The growing interest in extended producer responsibility

EPR is not a static concept, and the ways in which it is most effectively implemented are still being explored. Internationally, governments (and industry) are paying more attention to the relationship between regulations and innovation and the emergence of new competitive industries. Various approaches to EPR policy are being watched specifically because they appear to stimulate new innovation and business success as well as reduce overall life-cycle environmental impacts.

Many European policy-makers now refer to EPR as the product of a general evolution in approaches to dealing with pollution, waste and other environmental

---

4 The Environment Act containing the sections giving the UK government power to require producer responsibility for industry in relation to packaging and products was passed in July 1995.

issues. Concern over pollution and waste initially led to end-of-pipe approaches aimed at 'blocking' pollution (with targets and controls on factory emissions, higher costs for waste disposal, etc.). This has generated significant new markets in environmental technologies designed for 'cleaning up' waste (e.g. scrubbing, extracting, filtering) and monitoring waste levels.

This end-of-pipe approach was soon complemented by a more sophisticated interest in waste prevention and pollution minimisation. Internationally, this latter approach became known as 'cleaner production'. From this perspective, factories are no longer treated as discrete entities, the waste from which must be prevented from entering our air, water and land. The interest has shifted to redesigning or reconfiguring production processes to minimise resource consumption and waste. In most cases, this approach offers net, long-term economic, as well as environmental, gains, as the efficiency of the system is improved.

Cleaner production begins to link innovation, R&D and economics to the issue and value of improving environmental quality. However, cleaner production also needs to take into account other components of the system, beyond the factory. After all, the purpose of production is the creation and sale of new products, and their transportation, use and ultimate end-of-life disposal all contribute to a range of environmental impacts. The economics of a particular system of production, consumption and end-of-life disposal—its resource usage and its environmental and social outcomes—all derive from the specific characteristics of an industrial product: its material composition, its energy consumption, its mode of operation and so on.

As concern about waste, pollution and environmental degradation has grown, the market for consumer products has become sensitive to issues of environmental quality. Over the past decade or so manufacturers have been forced to respond to an increasingly sophisticated focus on the environmental impacts of products and a growing demand for 'greener' goods.

Various European countries introduced 'product-oriented policies'—measures aimed at 'closing the loop' in the production–consumption system, eliminating or reducing waste and pollution at all points in the chain (Cramer 1993). These include the introduction of resource taxes aimed at stimulating more resource-efficient production and the better utilisation of recycled materials (by improving their costs relative to virgin materials). They also include product stewardship or EPR.

1.5.4 The range of policies on extended producer responsibility in global markets

Ten OECD countries have legislation in place that provides for regulations, covenants, ordinances or other mechanisms to impose EPR for particular product categories (OECD 1997). Product categories currently included in, or targeted for, EPR programmes in OECD countries and in the European Communities (EC) include packaging, tyres, batteries, waste oil, chlorofluorocarbons (CFCs), printed matter, electrical and electronic products, office equipment, cars, furniture, building products and agricultural plastics.

A number of different policy tools are used or are under consideration by governments to implement EPR. These include deposit–refund schemes, product disposal charges, voluntary agreements or covenants with industry to achieve waste targets and end-of-life product take-back requirements. Environmental labelling, environmentally based procurement programmes and minimum recycled content requirements are also considered as part of the EPR policy armoury (see e.g. Davis 1995: 95-109).

1.5.4.1 Deposit–refund schemes

Denmark, Switzerland and Sweden have required makers and/or suppliers of small consumer batteries to levy a refundable deposit,[5] and Austria operates a similar policy for fluorescent lights and tyres. Korea has deposit–refund schemes covering beverage containers, batteries, tyres, televisions, washing machines and lubricating oils. Taiwan introduced a similar system for polyethylene terephthalate (PET) bottles in 1991 (OECD 1993).

1.5.4.2 Advance disposal fees

An advance deposit fee is set to a level estimated to cover real disposal or recovery costs and is paid by the producer into a government fund. A variation on this approach is that consumers who handle the waste from a product in a certain specified way receive a refund of the fee at the end of the product's life. In Austria this approach is used for refrigerators, and in Sweden it is used for automobiles. In 1993 the State of Florida in the USA imposed a 1% fee on containers that had not achieved a 50% recycling rate. This scheme raised over US$44 million in its first year of operation (for a review of this scheme, see Boehm and Hunt 1995: 12-13). Hawaii enacted a similar fee on glass containers. Some 21 US states have schemes for tyres, and 10 US states and most Canadian provinces have systems for beverage containers (Lifset 1995: 37-51).

1.5.4.3 Voluntary agreements and covenants

The UK Producer Responsibility Act 1995 essentially commits the government to negotiate with various industry sectors to achieve a waste reduction strategy acceptable to, and managed by, the industry. The Netherlands covenant system sets voluntary agreements within a framework of long-term targets and provisions for enforceable ordinances or regulations, should voluntary covenants fail to achieve the targets. A covenant on packaging wastes was the first result of the Netherlands approach; other agreements include one reached on automobiles, where the industry asked government to introduce a fee to support end-of-life recycling. This agreement is binding on all parties in the production chain. For

---

5   The scale and content of waste from batteries is illustrated by a 1993 German study: 800 million batteries were sold in Germany in that year, comprising 4,400 tonnes of zinc, 430 tonnes each of nickel and cadmium, 13 tonnes of mercury and 10 tonnes of silver. This represents almost a 100% increase over 1990 levels. In 1995 around 3 billion batteries were sold in the USA, most destined for landfill (*Warmer Bulletin UK* 45 [May 1995]: 23).

batteries, tyres and agricultural plastics, however, the Netherlands government legislated after it was clear that the industry sectors could not agree on a voluntary covenant. The Australian government has negotiated a voluntary packaging covenant with industry, supported by a legislative safety net to catch 'freeloaders'.

1.5.4.4 Product take-back systems

Product take-back involves the establishment of set targets for collection and recovery of products, with laws, regulations or ordinances setting out the responsibility of the individual producer or importer to 'take back and recover' their products unless certain other conditions are in place. Industry-wide schemes are generally allowed for. The best known of the product take-back systems relate to packaging, with the German Packaging Ordinance and its industry-wide scheme for collection and recycling—the Duales System Deutschland—being the most prominent and most studied.[6] The German system is credited with reducing packaging waste. Plastic waste fell from 923 thousand tonnes in 1991 to 823 thousand tonnes in 1995 and is now a significant source of new jobs. Some 18,000 jobs were created directly by the Duales System.[7]

1.6 The competitive edge: the greening of the market

In Australia, environmental protection is still viewed by some (vocal) parts of industry as just another potential burden that will increase costs and reduce profits. In the European context (and to a great extent in the USA and Japan), regulations and policies to increase environmental protection appear to have become a new stimulus for innovation and to have led companies to identify new business opportunities. Leading companies—such as Xerox, Electrolux, Bosch, BMW, Philips, Volvo, AEG and Wilkhahn—have invested heavily in new processes, systems, production technologies and design methods in the search for dramatic reductions in the environmental impacts of their products. Such companies decide to invest in this way because they:

- Want to position themselves as market leaders and innovators

- Do not want future 'surprises' (they want to 'anticipate' the changing regulatory and market context rather than to 'react' to changes as they are upon them)

6   This ordinance requires that waste from packaging be taken back by producers and re-used or recycled independent of the existing public waste-collection system. Retailers must take back primary sales packaging. Any secondary packaging used for safety or security may be left by consumers at retail shops or supermarkets. Transport or shipping packaging must be taken back by manufacturers or distributors.
7   As reported by Dr Helmut Schnurer of the German Ministry for Environment, at Green Goods 3, the third international conference on product-oriented environmental policy, Oslo, 15–17 February 1996, organised by the Norwegian Ministry of Environment.

- Recognise the emergence of a new business paradigm and a new competitive terrain
- Desire to act responsibly (to have a clear conscience on the part of directors)
- Desire to influence the direction of regulations and legislation (in partnership with government and to secure their investment)
- Desire to strengthen technical competence and develop new areas of technical competency ('handling environment')
- Want to change or improve the market image of the whole company

No business that strives to remain competitive, open to new markets and new opportunities can afford to ignore the global demands for environmental quality. The international market for low-impact products is growing at an astonishing rate. In established industrialised markets such as Europe, the USA, Canada and Japan, the demand for such products, and the investment to create them, is driven by increasingly stringent regulations and standards. In the rapidly developing economies of Asia, demand is growing because of resource constraints in those regions that would otherwise limit the rate of development. Demand for 'cleaner and greener' products is also growing because investment in research, design and innovation is delivering new competitive products with greatly improved environmental efficiencies.

Whether through the market pull of environmentally aware consumers, the corporate foresight of industry or the radical regulatory shifts imposed by governments, the global market for manufactured goods is unequivocally reconfiguring itself to meet key environmental imperatives, albeit at different speeds by different industry sectors.

More and more companies are openly proclaiming their environmental intentions and credentials, recognising that increasingly astute consumers are 'putting their money where their mouth is' when it comes to purchasing goods and services. Environmental issues no longer relate solely to compliance, clean-ups and other end-of-pipe scenarios. The days of companies acting on environmental issues simply because they are required to by government are going, especially among OECD nations. Furthermore, the recent phase of implementing cleaner production or pollution prevention as a way of saving money (and protecting the environment) has also been acknowledged as an incomplete solution to minimising environmental impacts.

Companies are realising that the 'environment' is a source of innovation in its own right and provides a unique opportunity to boost competitiveness. The commercial edge possible through eliminating or minimising undesirable environmental impacts through DfE not only helps in saving money via the old cleaner production process but also can directly contribute to making money in a responsible manner—if cleverly executed. In many ways, DfE embodies the attitude of 'work smarter not harder'.

Global companies with long histories wish to remain competitive for many years to come, despite the usual machinations of restructures, amalgamations, takeovers and collapses. These companies can see that growing consumer awareness about environmental degradation will continue to mature and gather momentum, as today's well-informed and eco-oriented youths become more affluent consumers in the 21st century. In this instance it is neither government regulation nor the availability of cleaner production technologies that are the corporate stimulant for pursuing product-oriented environmental initiatives.

Companies know that their own economic sustainability directly depends on having a healthier environment and thus a flourishing society to which a product may be marketed. Sustainable companies will rely on sustainable products and services both to meet the need of more demanding customers and to help find and embody that competitive edge over more conservative companies who treat environmental protection lightly and with apathy.

Probably the strongest testament to the greening of the international market is the expanding number of companies seriously addressing environmental aspects as part of their product development process. These companies are global players seeking to maximise profits in volatile markets, so their decision to integrate environmental objectives holistically across all company operations, services, processes and products was unlikely to have been taken casually, even if government regulations did provide an incentive in some cases.

Overall the message is clear—DfE has a critical role to play in making companies more profitable over and above the need for environmental compliance. Just as the intelligent and effective use of conventional design has successfully transformed companies and their products into trusted household names, the ability for DfE to play a similar role can reap brand loyalty, consumer respect and the resulting commercial gains that logically proceed from this. In Box 1.2 the list of companies allocating substantial resources to DfE initiatives not only demonstrates serious corporate environmental foresight but is also an acute reminder that the sceptics indifferent to DfE have got it wrong—and most likely at great financial loss over the longer term.

1.7 Summary

This chapter has set out to provide an overview of the who, where, what and why of DfE. In some ways this contextual chapter is a small-scale map in need of closer scrutiny, observation and action. It highlights some of the key players in, and drivers of, DfE and offers some snapshot definitions, directions and explanations.

Although this chapter may have raised more questions than it has answered, the reader will find that the 'hands-on' chapters to follow begin to illuminate the approaches, guidelines, methods and case studies that can maximise the life-cycle environmental performance of everyday products. As mentioned at the beginning, an important underlying philosophy of this book is to assist all those

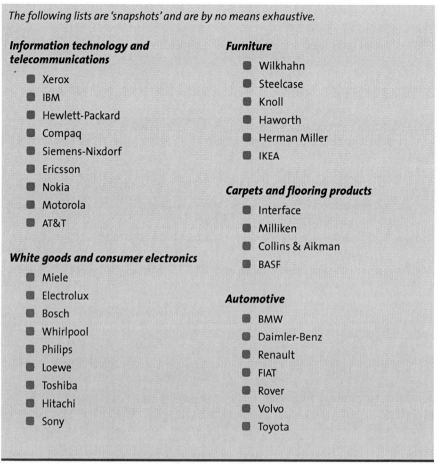

The following lists are 'snapshots' and are by no means exhaustive.

Information technology and telecommunications

- Xerox
- IBM
- Hewlett-Packard
- Compaq
- Siemens-Nixdorf
- Ericsson
- Nokia
- Motorola
- AT&T

White goods and consumer electronics

- Miele
- Electrolux
- Bosch
- Whirlpool
- Philips
- Loewe
- Toshiba
- Hitachi
- Sony

Furniture

- Wilkhahn
- Steelcase
- Knoll
- Haworth
- Herman Miller
- IKEA

Carpets and flooring products

- Interface
- Milliken
- Collins & Aikman
- BASF

Automotive

- BMW
- Daimler-Benz
- Renault
- FIAT
- Rover
- Volvo
- Toyota

Box 1.2 **A snapshot of companies pursuing cleaner and greener products**

involved in the product development process to better respond to environmental concerns without the need to become an 'environmental scientist' to do so.

Design is partly about problem-solving and therefore DfE is a very focused aspect of the process. However, design is also a highly creative human endeavour that can generate fun and desire while meeting the needs of society. In other words, avoid becoming a 'green and grumpy' designer and focus on how DfE can simultaneously fulfil the serious problem-solving aspects and the more whimsical and entertaining qualities associated with everyday products.

Above all, this chapter proposes a context within which design for environment has emerged, operates and evolves and thus a foundation from which to build and move onto action-oriented strategies and approaches that can be applied in practice.

MANAGING ECODESIGN

2.1 Overview of the design process

The methods outlined in this chapter are based on those used by the National Centre for Design at the Royal Melbourne Institute of Technology (RMIT) for the EcoReDesign™ programme (Gertsakis *et al.* 1997). Other methods and approaches have also been developed, for example by Brezet and van Hemel (1997). These and other useful publications are listed and described in the 'Further reading' section at the end of this chapter.

Ecodesign recognises that environmental impacts must be considered during the design process, along with all of the usual design criteria. It is therefore not a completely new process; it is simply a variation on the existing process. This chapter explains some of the methods and tools that other designers have found helpful. These are discussed as a series of five steps.

- Step 1: assess environmental impacts

- Step 2: research the market

- Step 3: run an ideas workshop

- Step 4: select design strategies

- Step 5: design the product

2.2 Assessing environmental impacts

One of the first steps in environmental design is an analysis of environmental impacts. One of the most useful tools for this is life-cycle assessment (LCA), which is a technique for assessing the environmental impacts associated with a product or service. Other techniques include the streamlined LCA and environmental matrix. These tools range in price and complexity and must be selected to match the goal, scope and budget of the project. A number of relevant tools are discussed in detail in Chapter 3.

The main objective in undertaking an environmental assessment is to identify the areas of greatest environmental impact so that these can be addressed through the design process. Sometimes the results of an environmental assessment are predictable: for example, finding that energy consumption is the cause of most impacts over the life-cycle of a washing machine. Others are less predictable, such as the discovery that one of the materials used in manufacture, albeit in small amounts, is highly toxic.

The environmental assessment will provide the designer with a sound basis for decision-making when developing the design brief (see Section 2.5). The assessment can be undertaken by technical or environmental staff within the company or by a specialist consulting group.

2.3 Researching the market

Prior to commencing the actual design process, the designer will need to undertake background research on the product, its competitors, developments in related products, any pressures for change and the market in general. This research will help to understand the requirements of the market and to identify any new ideas or technologies that could be pursued during the design process.

The results of this research should be compiled into a written report, or general product analysis (GPA). In addition to its value as an internal working document, a written report on the product will provide useful background information for participants in the ideas workshop (see Section 2.4). The product information—components, materials, production processes, etc.—is essential background information for the environmental assessment. For this reason the GPA and the environmental assessment may be undertaken concurrently.

The GPA would normally be prepared in-house, with input from staff in marketing, technical and corporate affairs departments. Some of the issues worth pursuing at this stage are listed in Box 2.1. The GPA will identify the current best environmental practice for the type of product being designed.

2.4 Running an ideas workshop

A workshop can be used to generate creative ideas and strategies. A group of between 8 and 15 people is the ideal number to encourage lively discussion between all participants. The group should be selected to provide diversity of skills and perspectives. It will be useful to include people with technical exper-

Product information

- A broad description of the product, its function and key components and of key design and production features

- A brief outline of the history of the product and its development over time (it is important not to assume that the 'evolution' of a product follows an improvement path, where each advance devalues all that has gone before; 'old' ideas can often take on a 'new' life because of changes in materials or production processes, or because of changes in social or cultural values)

- Manufacturers and sources of all components

- A list of all materials used in the product, the weight of each material and the source of each material

- A list of all production processes involved in fabricating the various components of the product

- Data on the (functional) use of the product, resources consumed (if any), frequency of use (if relevant), any emissions generated and expected average lifetime

Service and repair information.

- Current patterns of disposal of the product at end of life

Market information

- Key attributes of the product (e.g. functional, aesthetic, quality and cost attributes) considered to be important to market placement

- Current size of the market, including trends and future predictions

- Nature of the market—customers, niches, competition

- Other factors affecting market and product position—costs, regulations and standards, consumer interests

- Any environmental issues identified within the market

- Claims by competitors with regard to the environmental quality of similar products

Information on competing products

- History

- Recent design or development trends, particularly any trends in environmental features

Box 2.1 **Outline of a general product analysis (GPA)** *(continued over)*

Source: Gertsakis *et al.* 1997: 52

- ▣ Comparison of different environmental attributes across the total product range
- ▣ Identification (if relevant and possible) of the competing product (in the global market) with the best environmental profile

Information on the company: resources and capabilities

- ▣ Outline of the company—its history, size, facilities and resources
- ▣ Any environmental policy of the company or any history of environmental action or concern

Information on pressures or potential for change of product

- ▣ Environmental issues
- ▣ New materials
- ▣ New technologies
- ▣ New customer demands or niche markets

Information on developments in related products

It can stimulate 'design ideas' to list what is happening to products in other categories that could be considered as related in some way to the products concerned; for example:

- ▣ Products that occupy the same 'use space' (if the focus product is a domestic appliance, then what is happening to other domestic appliances in the same area of the home—say the kitchen?)
- ▣ Other products using the same materials or technology

Box 2.1   *(continued)*

tise relevant to the product: for example, energy efficiency or recycling. Key people from the company should be included, from management, design, production, environment, marketing and servicing. It may also be beneficial to include a good lateral thinker—preferably someone outside the design team who can ask obscure or unexpected questions that might lead to creative solutions. A good facilitator is, of course, essential.

A simple agenda for the workshop is presented in Box 2.2, although this may need to be modified to suit individual company or product circumstances.

A number of creative tools are available to assist in identifying and evaluating ideas. Creative tools are not unique to design or design for environment (DfE), and there are substantial texts on development of creative group processes. What we present here are a couple of creative tools—brainstorming and use of sticky labels—that are commonly used for DfE workshops.

General product analysis

- Present results
- Invite questions and discussion
- Identify key opportunities and/or threats

Environmental assessment

- Present results
- Invite questions and discussion
- Identify key impacts (one may wish to rank them according to severity of impact, social or political importance, regulatory threats, profile in the market, etc.)

Design strategies

- Hold a creative brainstorming session (no constraints)
- List ideas and strategies on a whiteboard or similar

Review of ideas/strategies (optional)

- Hold a critical reflection on the above ideas, looking at feasibility and applicability
- Identify priorities

Box 2.2 **Agenda for an ideas workshop**

- Brainstorming became a bit of a cliché activity through the 1990s; however, it is still a useful tool for getting ideas out of people's minds and 'onto the table' for consideration. A question or problem is posed to a group (often in a workshop situation) and people are given a set period to raise all and any potential solutions or ideas relating to the problem. The ideas are recorded on a whiteboard or a large piece of paper; no judgement or critique is made of the ideas as they are being recorded. Once the time is up, usually between two and five minutes, ideas are discussed and clarified. Scores may then be assigned to the ideas based on their practicality or effectiveness. It is often in this discussion phase that ideas that appear completely impractical can lead to valuable insights.

- The use of sticky labels is a similar process to brainstorming; however, it aims to involve all participants, some of whom remain quiet throughout open brainstorming sessions. Each participant is given a set number of sticky labels (Post-It™ notes work well). A problem or issue is put to the group and each participant in asked to write down, without discussion, five possible solutions to the problem. These solutions may be recorded graphically or through simple descriptions. By forcing each person to raise a set number of responses—say five—the well of the creative subconscious is, one hopes, tapped from each person. Each person places his or her notes on a wall together with those of the other participants, so that all participants can view all the ideas. The ideas are then grouped together by the participants, still without any discussion. Each participant can group any of the ideas in whatever way he or she sees it as being relevant to the problem. The labels may be regrouped by another participant, and this process continues iteratively until the group is happy with the result. The grouped ideas can then be discussed and prioritised in the same way as in the brainstorm.

The workshop will normally generate a range of good ideas, and some of these might be selected for inclusion in the design brief. This process can be particularly useful in generating 'leapfrog' solutions that may not emerge through the normal, incremental design process. It can help designers and engineers to think 'outside the square'.

In planning the workshop, one will need to consider:

- Finding a good working space

- Locating necessary audiovisual equipment, such as an overhead projector or an electronic whiteboard

- Paying fees for the facilitator and outside participants (if required)

- Appointing a 'scribe' to record outcomes

Workshops can be a vital tool for generating creative solutions to design problems and at the same time building in ownership of the process across different sections of an organisation. An ideas workshop is useful in the early stages of the design process; however, creative group work can be used at many different stages of the DfE project.

2.4.1 Assessing the outcomes of the workshop

The workshop will generally have concluded with some critical evaluation of the 'value' of various ideas generated in response to the environmental profile of the product. However, it is often better to set aside a later session to review the whole workshop outcomes and develop a brief for the new, improved, product.

The first task of the review process is to collate the workshop material into a hierarchy of four groups of ideas, concepts or strategies (see also Fig. 2.1):

- Category 1: those that appear to achieve significant environmental gains and that are technically and economically feasible

- Category 2: those that appear to achieve limited environmental gains but that are technically and economically feasible

- Category 3: those that appear to achieve significant environmental gains but that are questionable in terms of their technical or economic feasibility

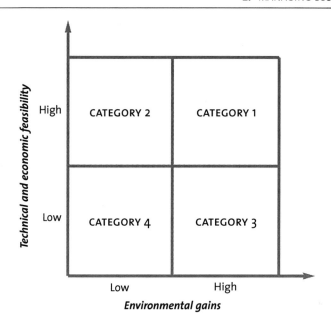

Figure 2.1 **Categorisation of workshop outcomes**

■ Category 4: those that appear to achieve limited environmental gains and that are technically or economically questionable

The determination of this hierarchy is the first step towards preparing a brief.

How far down that hierarchy a company is willing to proceed will depend on how much can be achieved in the short term and on the level of resources and time available to undertake longer-term research and development. This will depend, in turn, on the urgency of the company's product development cycle and the demand for the improved product.

Those ideas and concepts that fall into category 1 above can clearly be implemented in the short term. As many ideas and concepts as possible from category 2 should also be included in any short-term plans. Generally, proposals that fall into category 4 can be discarded. The review process has then to determine how many of the propositions falling into category 3 should be further researched before a brief is developed.

The second task for the review process is to consider each of the proposals that fall into categories 1, 2 and 3 to check for any conflicting directions. Although the workshop process will often draw out any ideas that are in conflict with one another, this is such an important issue that it should be reviewed again, carefully. The most significant problem for the DfE process is that a design decision that reduces the environmental impacts in one area can increase the impacts in another. For example:

- Replacing steel with aluminium may reduce the carbon dioxide (CO_2) levels from transport (by reducing the weight of the product), but it can also increase the CO_2 produced in processing and manufacture because of the high input of electricity required to process bauxite into aluminium

- Prolonging the life of a product may delay improvements in its efficiency, unless it is designed for the upgrading of components (new appliances are often more efficient to use than previous models)

There is no simple system for identifying or resolving such conflicts, although some of the LCA tools presented in Chapter 3 may help. It is just another example of the 'backwards and forwards' checking process, testing each proposition to see that it does not have unwanted effects elsewhere.

Some proposals can also be prioritised based on the new features or advantages that they bring to the product.

2.5 Selecting design strategies

On the basis of all of this information—the environmental assessment, GPA and workshop review—design strategies can be selected for inclusion in the brief. These strategies may include:

- Selecting environmentally low-impact materials

- Avoiding toxic or hazardous materials

- Choosing cleaner production processes

- Maximising energy efficiency in manufacture and use

- Maximising water efficiency in use

- Designing for waste minimisation

These general strategies are discussed in Chapter 4, and more product-specific guidelines are provided at the end of Chapter 6 (packaging), Chapter 7 (textiles and clothing), Chapter 8 (furniture) and Chapter 9 (appliances).

The design brief should clearly outline the company's requirements for the new or improved product. A suggested structure for the brief is included in Box 2.3.

At this stage of the process one may also need to undertake or commission more specific research on materials or technologies—for example on:

- The availability of particular recycled materials that meet performance standards

- The latest developments in efficient electric motors

- Replacements for ozone-depleting chemicals

Introduction

- Define the aim of the design project
- List specific objectives (e.g. 'to minimise environmental impacts of the product', 'to meet new regulatory standards', 'to achieve a six-star energy rating', 'to position the product as market leader')

General requirements

- Define the primary function of the product
- State the durability requirements
- List aesthetic considerations
- Define ergonomics requirements
- List the safety requirements and issues
- Outline the required performance and quality

Environmental objectives

- List specific strategies relating to materials, efficiency, recovery at end of life and so on
- Include quantitative targets where relevant (e.g. 'use 50% recycled material', 'design for recycling in the post-consumer HDPE [high-density polyethylene] stream')

Production requirements

- Specify manufacturing requirements or limitations
- Include any objectives or targets (e.g. 'minimise components to streamline assembly process')

Regulations and standards

- List any mandatory regulations, standards or codes of practice relevant to the product

Cost

- Specify limits on cost of production to ensure that the product is competitive (e.g. 'product must be manufactured in Australia for less than Aus$100 per unit')

Box 2.3 **Outline of a design brief**

2.6 Designing the product

The actual design process can involve many stages, including:

- Preparation of concepts
- Detailed design
- Production of prototypes
- Testing
- Final design

After completion of each stage, the design team will need to evaluate progress and make decisions about how to proceed. This process will include an evaluation against the design brief, including performance requirements, environmental objectives, production issues and cost.

◢ Further reading

Bakker, C., *Environmental Information for Industrial Designers* (self-published PhD dissertation; Rotterdam, 1995; e-mail: conny@knoware.nl).

> This is a good source for anyone interested in ecodesign, design tools and process and how they relate to environmental information needs.

Bor, A., and G. Blom, *Introduction to Environmental Product Development* (Eindhoven, Netherlands: European Design Centre, 1994).

> This is an excellent introduction to the practice of environmentally oriented product development. It includes case studies, illustrations and an overview of the key issues.

Brezet, H., and C. van Hemel, *Ecodesign: A Promising Approach to Sustainable Production and Consumption* (Paris: United Nations Environment Programme, 1997).

> This is a practical guide to ecodesign based on the results of a Dutch demonstration programme.

Burall, P., *Product Development and the Environment* (Aldershot, UK: Gower Publishing, 1996).

> This is a practical guide for managers and designers seeking to develop efficient and clean products. It covers various design tools, management and marketing issues and strategies for blending the technical, the commercial and the environmental.

Fiksel, J., *Design for Environment* (New York: McGraw–Hill, 1996).

> This is a lengthy text that discusses how 'design for environment' can provide a highly effective life-cycle approach to new product and process development. It takes into account the environment, human health and safety. Overall, it is a very comprehensive and detailed guide with practical suggestions for diverse industries.

Gertsakis, J., H. Lewis and C. Ryan, *A Guide to EcoReDesign™* (Melbourne: Centre for Design, Royal Melbourne Institute of Technology, 1997).

> This is a practical guide to ecodesign methods and strategies, with a series of case studies from the EcoReDesign™ programme at RMIT.

3
ENVIRONMENTAL ASSESSMENT TOOLS

3.1 Introduction

Like any trade, design for environment (DfE) has a set of tools that are available to make the job more thorough and reliable and to short-cut some of the difficult tasks that are otherwise too expensive and impractical to undertake on each job. However, like all tools they are open to misuse and misinterpretation. This chapter outlines the major tools available for use in DfE, and where and when they are best applied.

The tools fall into two broad groups: analytical and creative. Tools from each of these areas need to be used iteratively in the search for solutions and new directions. The aim of this chapter is to outline some of the analytical tools available to assist in the identification and evaluation of environmental impacts.

As each tool is discussed, the tools are scored in terms of their cost (both the purchase cost and the time needed to use the tool), simplicity of use and overall effectiveness in providing useful and reliable information for the design process. The scoring is based on a scale of one to five ticks, with one being a very poor rating and five being excellent. This is a rough guide based on the experience of the authors and will vary over time as the tools are refined.

The main aim of the analytical tools in DfE is to gain insights into environmental impacts throughout the life-cycle of the product or service. The importance of life-cycle thinking has been covered in Chapter 1. Analysis of the life-cycle of a product or service involves looking towards the past, or upstream processes, of the product or service (raw materials, manufacturing, transport and so on) and looking to the future use and possible disposal options, or downstream processes, of the product (energy and materials consumed by the product in use, re-use, recycling or disposal option for the product).

Life-cycle assessment (LCA) has become as much a way of thinking as a specific tool or methodology. As a concept, LCA attempts to attribute the environmental loads from all stages of the life-cycle of a product or product system back to the 'functional unit' of the product (see Fig. 3.1). This allows the product designer to consider and design around the broader environmental implications of the product.

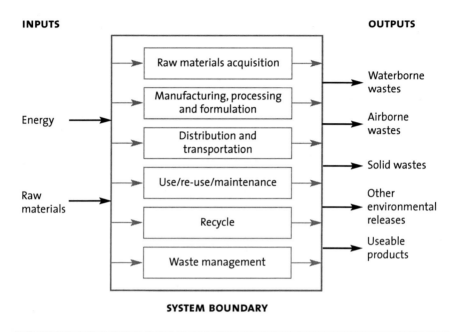

Figure 3.1 **Product system from a life-cycle perspective**

Source: SETAC 1992: xix

However, although LCA can be seen as a concept or an approach, the term has stricter application as a specific and internationally standardised methodology for assessing environmental burdens from product systems. (For this reason a range of terms such as life-cycle thinking, life-cycle approach and streamlined LCA are used for the broader concepts and associated tools spawned by LCA.)

Although full LCA, undertaken in accordance with internationally recognised methods, is not the most common tool for DfE, it does underpin many of the other tools and is therefore covered first in this section.

3.2 Life-cycle assessment

The LCA methodology has developed over the past two decades, predominantly in Europe but also in the USA and more recently Asia. The internationally agreed standard for LCA has been developed by the

Tool scores	
Cost	✓
Simplicity	✓✓
Effectiveness	✓✓✓✓

International Organisation for Standardisation (ISO), and this is documented in four environmental management system standards (the ISO 14000 series). The methodology is generally broken up into four stages:

- Definition of the goal and scope

- Life-cycle inventory analysis

- Life-cycle impact assessment

- Life-cycle interpretation

3.2.1 Definition of the goal and scope

This first stage is very important as it defines the questions being asked in the LCA and the scope of the activities that will be undertaken to answer those questions. The goal and scope also define the boundaries of the systems that will be included in the assessment. The goal and scope can be revisited later in the project in light of new information or in light of a lack of available information. An example of defining the goal and scope for a polystyrene cup is shown in Fig. 3.2.

3.2.2 Life-cycle inventory analysis

To determine the impact of a product on the environment it is necessary to determine the flows of material and energy through the product system. Individual elements of the system, or unit processes, are analysed to determine the use of energy and materials and the emission of pollutants. The unit processes are linked together to form the product system, and the flows of materials are calculated for the product. The result of this analysis is a long list of resources used and emissions to the environment (air, water, soil, etc.). On its own, this data may contain some useful information, such as total carbon dioxide (CO_2) emissions, or the total emissions of a controlled substance. However, this data generally needs further analysis and grouping to provide useful indicators that can be used for decision-making. An example of inventory results for the design of a polystyrene cup is shown in Table 3.1.

3.2.3 Life-cycle impact assessment

This stage takes the list of numbers provided by the inventory and classifies them into different environmental impact categories. These categories are defined in the goal and scope and usually include common impacts such as global warming, energy use, solid waste and toxic emissions (see Chapter 5 for more information on the environmental impacts of products). Relevant inventory results are attributed to different impact categories (Fig. 3.3). Some indicators have very reliable information on how the emissions affect the impact category (e.g. CO_2 affects global warming by a factor of 1; methane affects global warming by a factor of

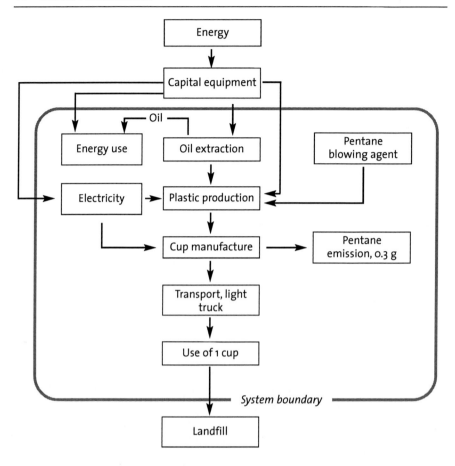

Goal: to determine the main environmental impacts of the polystyrene cup, and the stages of the life-cycle where they occur.

Scope *(Australian situation):* include all material production stages, transport and use, excluding data on capital equipment and final disposal of cup.

Figure 3.2 **Life-cycle assessment: example of the goal and scope for a polystyrene cup**

22). However, for many impacts this information is not available or reliable (e.g. in the case of toxic emissions).

Impact results can be 'normalised' to determine equivalent contributions within each category compared with a national or global reference value. The categories can then be weighted based on their environmental significance. The weighted impact can then be summed to determine a single score or 'eco-indicator'. These steps require many subjective judgements and are an area of significant debate

Raw materials

Substance	Unit	
Bauxite (ore)	mg	35.2
Clay	μg	440
Coal	g	2.39
Crude oil	g	26.3
Iron (ore)	mg	9.94
Limestone rock	mg	19.8
Natural gas	dm³	22.4
Rock salt	mg	26.4
Water	cm³	183

Airborne emissions

Substance	Unit	
Aldehydes	ng	45.3
Aluminium	μg	6.95
Ammonia	μg	2.09
Carbon dioxide (CO$_2$)	g	77.4
Carbon monoxide (CO)	mg	189
Copper	μg	3.49
Dioxin	pg	0.973
Dust	mg	124
Ethanol	ng	695
Ethene	μg	27.8
Ethyl benzene	μg	13.9
Formaldehyde	μg	2.78
Halon-1301	g	2.09
Hydrocarbons (C$_x$H$_y$)	mg	509
Iron	μg	6.95
Methane	mg	74.9
Methane	mg	2.74
Methanol	μg	1.39
Magnesium	μg	2.09
Nickel	μg	13.9
Nitrogen oxides:		
N$_2$O	μg	286
NO$_2$	mg	2.87
NO$_x$	g	1.02
PAH[a]	μg	1.32
Pentane	g	1.45
Propane	μg	556
Propene	μg	27.8
Radioactive substances	Bq	792
Silicates	μg	13.9
Soot	kg	32.8
Sulphide (H$_2$S)	μg	111
Sulphur oxides (SO$_x$)	g	3.25
Toluene	μg	195
Vanadium	μg	55.6
VOC[b]	mg	57.7
Zinc	μg	8.34

Waterborne emissions

Substance	Unit	
Acid[c]	μg	1.76
Aluminium	μg	243
Ammonia	mg	9.45
Arsenic	ng	695
Barium	μg	973
Benzene	μg	50.7
BOD[d]	mg	2.68
Boron	μg	13.9
Calcium	mg	13.4
Chlorine (Cl$_2$)	mg	2.2
Chlorine ions (C$^-$)	mg	207
COD[e]	mg	60.5
Copper	μg	2.09
Cyanide	μg	2.09
Dissolved organics	mg	7.04
Dissolved solids	mg	8.68
Hydrocarbons (C$_x$H$_y$)	mg	15.3
Lead	μg	2.78
Magnesium	μg	799
Manganese	μg	27.8
Molybdenum	ng	695
Nickel	μg	2.09
Nitrogen	mg	1.26
As nitrate	μg	250
Total	μg	4.7
PAH[a]	μg	4.87
Phenol	μg	48.7
Phosphate	μg	20.9
Radioactive substances	Bq	7.3
Sodium	mg	126
Sulphate	mg	8.2
Suspended solids	mg	50.3

Solid emissions

Substance	Unit	
Chemical waste	mg	154
Diesel oil sludge	μg	308
Dust[f]	mg	21.3
Final waste (inert)	μg	577
Industrial waste	mg	9.5
Inorganic (general)	kg	0.0423
Mineral waste	mg	242
Product waste (active)	kg	0.00077
Slag	mg	76.6

a Polycyclic aromatic hydrocarbons
b Volatile organic compounds, excluding methane
c As H$^+$
d Biochemical oxygen demand
e Chemical oxygen demand
f Not specified

Note that this data is for illustrative purposes only and should not be taken as actual data for a polystyrene cup. The large number of inventory entries provide little useful information for decision-making. The next stage of the LCA groups the data into indicators or 'impact categories'.

Table 3.1 **Life-cycle assessment: example of inventory results for a polystyrene cup**

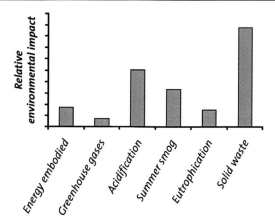

These results have been normalised (compared to a reference value such as total yearly impact for each impact). Categories can also be weighted and summed together to form an eco-indicator.

Figure 3.3 **Impact assessment results**

within the LCA community. However, for users with little time and environmental knowledge, single scores based on impact weighting represent useful information that can readily be used in the decision-making process.

3.2.4 *Life-cycle interpretation*

In the life-cycle interpretation phase significant results from the LCA are tested to check their validity before making and reporting the conclusions. This is an extremely important step, given that LCA conclusions are the result of many calculations and assumptions. Where significant results are based on data that is not reliable, or on assumptions for which there is no verification, either more investigation is required or some form of qualification may need to be included when reporting the results. An example of the interpretation of an LCA for a polystyrene cup is shown in Table 3.2.

The current limitations of LCA are its inability to incorporate the complex range of environmental impacts that result from modern industrial activity. This is particularly so in the case of impacts on land and biodiversity and, to a lesser degree, eco-toxicity. LCA is most applicable to global indicators such as global warming, and less applicable to local impacts such as smog, where the timing and location of the emissions are more important. Despite these limitations, LCA is one of the best tools for allocating environmental responsibility from production systems back to the products and services that use them.

For a detailed overview of LCA methods there are good publications from the Society for Environmental Toxicology and Chemistry (SETAC 1992), the United

Significant issues	Checks required	Possible conclusion/ recommendation
High proportion of solid waste generated in moulding cup	Is all this material sent to landfill or is a proportion recovered?	Investigate greater recycling option for scrap
Summer smog is also a significant issue, from fugitive emissions in plastic production.	Check recent fugitive emission data, as significant improvements have been made recently in petrochemical industry. Are releases in smog-prone areas?	May be worth testing against alternate material such as paper cup
Acidification result is from sulphur released in energy production and refining.	Is sulphur data correct for Australia? Is acidification an issue in Australia and what are the main causes?	Investigate low-sulphur or green power alternatives if issue remains significant

Table 3.2 **Example of the interpretation of a life-cycle assessment (LCA) for a polystyrene cup**

Nations Environment Programme (UNEP 1996), the Centre for Environmental Science (CML 1995), Leiden University, the Netherlands, and Dr Bo Weidema's book on the environmental assessment of products (Weidema 1998). The LCA standards being produced by ISO as part of the ISO 14000 series of environmental management standards (the ISO 14040 series) are also a good guide to current LCA methodology, explaining many of the commonly used terms and providing examples.[1]

3.3 Streamlined life-cycle assessment

Owing to the costs and time constraints that are associated with full LCA studies, a range of streamlined LCA methods have been developed. In the context of DfE, the aim of a streamlined LCA is to:

- Identify the major environmental impacts of a product throughout its life-cycle

- Determine the environmental priorities that should be addressed through the design process

1   Visit www.iso.ch.

There are many approaches to streamlined LCA, from omitting specific system elements or reducing the number of indicators used, through to more qualitative approaches. Two methods are covered below in detail: a matrix-based approach and a software-based method. Streamlined tools may be used as a precursor to a more detailed LCA study.

3.3.1 Matrix-based life-cycle assessment

The approach used for a streamlined LCA is similar to the four-step process in a full LCA (Table 3.3). Possible equivalent processes for streamlined and full LCA are shown below.

Tool scores	
Cost	✓✓✓✓
Simplicity	✓✓✓
Effectiveness	✓✓

Full LCA	Streamlined or simplified LCA
Goal, scope and definition	Flowchart or process tree, with a design or product development brief
Inventory of all processes, with data taken back to basic materials (e.g. ores, coal, oil, CO_2, NO_x)	Inventory matrix usually includes the materials and flows directly connected to the product (e.g. polystyrene, propene, fugitive emissions)
Impact assessment	Impact assessment matrix
Interpretation	Design strategies and practicality versus efficacy matrix

Table 3.3 **Comparison of full life-cycle assessment (LCA) versus matrix-based, streamlined LCA**

3.3.1.1 Process tree

A process tree or life-cycle map can be used to assist in identifying all the key stages in the product life-cycle. The process tree should identify all the major upstream stages, such as raw material extraction and processing, and all the major downstream stages, such as packaging, distribution, transport, use, disposal and recycling.

The simple act of developing a process tree can be useful to alert people working in product development, design and marketing of the 'environmental baggage' associated with the product. An example of a process tree for a polystyrene cup is shown in Figure 3.4.

3.3.1.2 Inventory analysis matrix

The inventory matrix is a list of materials and energy used by the product throughout its life-cycle and the associated emissions arising from that product. It generally includes:

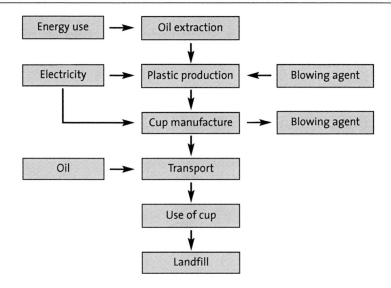

The detail will depend on the focus for the DfE project and the expertise available to develop the tree.

Figure 3.4 **Example of a process tree for a polystyrene cup**

- *Materials*
  - What materials are used?
  - What quantities are used?
  - Are there any significant impacts of individual materials?
- *Energy*
  - How much energy is consumed in manufacture?
  - What feedstock is used (coal, gas, oil, etc.)?
  - How is the product transported, and how far?
- *Wastes and emissions*
  - What wastes and emissions are produced?
  - Are any of them toxic or hazardous?

The focus of the information in the inventory matrix may be predominantly data available to the company for on-site impacts; however, it is useful to estimate some of the off-site impacts. An example of an inventory matrix for a polystyrene cup is shown in Table 3.4.

3.3.1.3 Impact assessment matrix

Impact assessment aims to simplify the inventory information into groups of emissions or potential impacts on the environment. Typical indicators used for impact assessment are:

	Input of materials	Energy use	Wastes and emissions
Production of basic materials	Expanded polystyrene, 18 g Propene, 2 g	Significant energy is used in the production of all basic materials.	VOCs (volatile organic compounds)
Manufacturing	Blowing agent, HFCs (hydrofluorocarbons)	Small energy use in cup manufacture	Emission of blowing agent
Distribution	Transport packaging for cups (2,000-cup boxes made from recycled paperboard weighing 200 g)	Transport is a small truck across metropolitan areas.	Emissions from transport include CO_2, NO_x and ozone.
Product use	Good thermal properties may prolong the time for which the drink is palatable, thus reducing use of additional materials for replacement coffee or tea, etc.	Good thermal properties may prolong the time for which the drink is palatable, thus reducing energy used in making replacement coffee or tea, etc.	Negligible
End of product life	Negligible	Small transport component to landfill	All cups end up as solid waste; there are also problems with litter.

Table 3.4 **Example of an inventory matrix for a polystyrene cup**

- Resource depletion (use of fossil fuels, minerals and ores)
- Global warming (owing to emissions of CO_2, methane, N_2O, chlorofluoro-carbons [CFCs])
- Smog (NO_x, non-methane volatile organic compounds [VOCs])
- Acidification (from acid gases)
- Eutrophication (the nutrient load in waterways leading to algal blooms, caused by NO_3, PO_4 and some airborne NO_x and PO_x)
- Toxic waste (may include both human and eco-toxic substances)
- Biodiversity reduction (not used in quantitative LCA work)

The impact assessment matrix draws on the information in the inventory matrix, identifying the potential impacts that may result from the significant inventory entries. For example, the inventory entry of blowing agent in cup manufacture is recorded in the impact matrix as impacts on summer smog, and emission of solid waste may have an impact on biodiversity (Table 3.5). One of the advantages of the matrix approach is that it is not limited to the quantifiable impacts, as is a full LCA. Indicators can be based on qualitative information.

	Resource depletion	Global warming	Smog	Acidifi- cation	Eutrophi- cation	Toxic waste	Biodiversity reduction
Production of basic materials	3[a]	3[b]	2[c]	1[d]	2[e]	2	2[f]
Manu- facturing	0	0	2[g]	1	1	1	0
Distri- bution	1	1	1	1	0	0	0
Product use	−1[h]	−1[h]	0	0	0	0	0
End of product life	0	0	0	0	0	0	1[i]
	3	3	5	3	3	3	3

Note: Impacts have been ranked from 0 (no impact) to 4 (maximum impact). A negative number may be used for a beneficial impact. The rules for the matrix are very loose and should be adapted to suit the product and company in question.

a   Oil resources limited in the long term
b   Methane emission from venting in oil production
c   Non-methane volatile organic compounds from venting and flaring
d   Low-sulphur oils used in Australia
e NO_x emission from energy use
f   Oil pollution
g   Emission of propene when moulding cup
h   Possible benefits in use
i   Impact of landfill and littering impacts

Table 3.5 **Example of an impact assessment matrix for the production of a polystyrene cup**

The information entered in the matrix can be qualitative or may include a ranking of the impact. The results of such a ranking exercise reflects the knowledge and experience of the person or team undertaking the exercise. It is important, therefore, to have a range of expertise available to rank the impacts at each life-cycle stage. To add guidance and consistency to the process, the rankings can be defined in general terms, such as:

0   No apparent impact

1   Small impact; no serious consequences

2   Significant impact; of some concern

3   Serious impact; a defining feature of the process or product

4   Very serious impact; highly regulated release; known to be causing significant environmental damage

The benefits of the weighting exercise are that numeric comparisons can be made between different design options. An example of such a comparative exercise is shown in Table 3.6.

Impact	Existing cup	New cup
Resource depletion	5	6
Global warming	7	3
Smog	5	5
Acidification	3	2
Eutrophication	3	2
Toxic waste	3	4
Biodiversity reduction	3	2

It is important not to sum the results of the different impact categories as this involves the assumption that each category is of equal importance. It is more beneficial to identify the significant impacts from each product and address them individually in the design.

Table 3.6 **Comparison of impact matrix results for the manufacture of a polystyrene cup**

3.3.1.4 Prioritising design options

On the basis of all of this information—the process tree, the inventory matrix and the impact assessment matrix—design strategies can be selected. These strategies can be prioritised by using a matrix with feasibility on one axis and the scale of potential improvement on the other, as shown in Table 3.7 for a polystyrene cup redesign.

3.3.1.5 The MECO matrix: an alternative matrix approach

Once users have a familiarity with LCA, the two-step matrix approach described above can be simplified into a simpler matrix. Weidema (1998) uses a MECO (materials–energy–chemicals–other) matrix in which major issues or flows are categorised and prioritised on a single matrix of life-cycle stages. Four impact categories as shown in Table 3.8.

	Environmental improvement		
	Large	**Moderate**	**Small**
Highly feasible		Lightweight cup	
May be feasible		CO_2 blowing agent	Energy recovery from waste cups
Not currently feasible	Use 100% recycled polymer	Recycling polystyrene	

Table 3.7 **Prioritisation matrix for the manufacture of a polystyrene cup**

	Materials	*Energy*	*Chemicals*	*Other*
Raw materials				
Production				
Use				
Disposal				

Table 3.8 **A MECO (materials–energy–chemicals–other) matrix**

3.3.2 Software-based life-cycle assessment

Tool scores	
Cost	✓✓✓*
Simplicity	✓✓✓
Effectiveness	✓✓✓✓

* *Initial software cost may be high; however, ongoing cost is lower.*

With the advent of computer models for LCA that are supported by large material and processes databases it has become possible to undertake 'quick and dirty' assessments of new products. These assessments can vary from a ten-minute analysis on two alternative materials, right through to the full LCA assessment described earlier.

The 'quick and dirty' LCA generally borrows data from existing databases, without detailed checks on the validity of its use. Assumptions and estimations are used to fill gaps in the data, with the main aim being to identify some potential priority areas for further investigation.

These quick software-based assessments can be a great aid to other design workshops and matrix-based tools. Although they lack data quality they do give some quantified results for the design process that can be verified with more detailed research.

There is a large range of software tools available for product design and LCA. These tools can incorporate large databases on the environmental profiles of materials, energy and transport systems. Although this allows the user to undertake detailed assessments, the assumptions behind the data are not always clear. A summary of some of the tools is presented in Table 3.9.

Tool	Examples	Comments
LCA modelling tools	SimaPro TEAM Gabi Umberto PEMS Boustead	These tools come with detailed databases from many sources and also allow users to input their own unit process data. They are excellent analytical tools and generally have a range of impact assessment models. The data, however, is mostly of European origin. The cost ranges from around Aus$2,000 to Aus$25, 000. Note that different models are available for different countries and industry sectors.
Product assessment models	EcoIT Ecoscan Idemat	These models draw on detailed data, but generally do not allow the user to specify new inventories. They focus on the product design and represent environmental impacts with a simple eco-point score. They range in price from Aus$100 to Aus$1,000. Some of these programmes can draw their data directly from detailed LCA programmes such as SimaPro.
Process assessment models	P2Edge	These models use data and process information to alert the user to cleaner production and to design improvement opportunities.

Table 3.9 **Life-cycle assessment (LCA) software tools**

Demonstration versions and software suppliers are available on the Internet at www.ecosite.co.uk or at www.sbi.se/orlando/lca-soft.htm.

3.4 Proxy indicators

Proxy indicators are single values that are used to represent the environmental impact of a product or material. Examples of proxy indicators include:

Tool scores	
Cost	✓✓✓
Simplicity	✓✓✓
Effectiveness	✓✓

- Embodied energy
- Material input per unit of service (MIPS), and 'ecological rucksacks'
- Ecological footprints
- Eco-indicators

3.4.1 Embodied energy

Embodied energy is the most commonly available indicator, and it has been applied extensively in the building industry. Data on embodied energy is often developed by using input–output analysis, which uses national economic data to determine

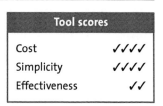

Tool scores	
Cost	✓✓✓✓
Simplicity	✓✓✓✓
Effectiveness	✓✓

the flow of energy through the economy. Embodied energy data for building materials has been developed for most common building and packaging materials in Australia, although the data can be variable (Trelour 1994). Embodied energy is a good indicator for systems that are dominated by energy use, such as many manufactured building materials. However, for natural materials such as timber, which has ecological impacts on land and biodiversity, with relatively low production energy, embodied energy is a very poor indicator.

3.4.2 Material input per unit of service, and 'ecological rucksacks'

Ecological rucksacks and the MIPS measure the total material inputs and transformations that result from products. MIPS was developed initially in Germany at the Wuppertal Institute for Climate,

Tool scores	
Cost	✓✓
Simplicity	✓
Effectiveness	✓✓

Environment and Energy (Schmidt-Bleek 1998). It overcomes some of the issues of embodied energy by accounting for all materials movements (not just those associated with energy content); however, it does not discriminate very well between different materials consumed or transformed.

3.4.3 Ecological footprints

Ecological footprints measure the total land area required to support the production of a service, product or lifestyle. This is a useful measure as it can be used to estimate the sustainability of particular activities for a given land area. Ecological

Tool scores	
Cost	✓✓✓
Simplicity	✓
Effectiveness	✓✓

footprints have been calculated for typical citizens of different countries around the world (Wackernagel 1997). It is then a simple calculation to multiply the total population by the available land to determine how close a society is to achieving a sustainable consumption level.

The problems with the ecological footprint are lack of data and its inability to account for variables not related to land area.

3.4.4 Eco-indicators

Eco-indicators are generally recognised as proxy indicators, as they are an attempt to model a wide

Tool scores	
Cost	✓✓✓*
Simplicity	✓✓
Effectiveness	✓✓

* Cost will be dependent on the availability of pre-calculated value for the products or materials of interest.

range of impacts that are then weighted against each other and summed into a single value. Because of the limitations in the science used to measure environmental impacts, and because of the value judgements built into weighting different impact categories, it is more useful to see these values as indicators or proxies for environmental impact rather than as a measure of any actual environmental impact.

3.4.4.1 Eco-points

One of the first attempts to develop a multi-point impact model appears to be the eco-points method developed by the Swiss Environment Agency (Bundesamt für Umwelt, Wald und Landschaft (Switzerland [BUWAL]) in 1990. It is based on a

Tool scores	
Cost	✓✓✓
Simplicity	✓✓
Effectiveness	✓✓

range of indicators (14 in all) that are weighted and aggregated based on how close the current emission levels are to Swiss government target levels. The further the indicator is from reaching its target, the greater the weighting (Ahbe *et al.* 1990). This is a good approach but it is very specific to Swiss policy and emission levels. It also fails to account for emissions produced outside Switzerland in other areas with different environmental sensitivities.

3.4.4.2 EPS

The EPS (environmental priority strategies in product development) method was developed in Sweden in the early 1990s and uses economic values to weigh up different impact categories. It looks at five 'safeguard' subjects: human health, biological diversity,

Tool scores	
Cost	✓✓
Simplicity	✓✓
Effectiveness	✓✓

production (i.e. fertility), resources and aesthetic values. Monetary values have been determined for each area by using actual expenditure or contingent valuation (willingness to pay; Steen and O'Ryding 1991). The EPS method was updated in 2000 and is available at www.pre.nl/simapro/impact_assessment_methods.htm#EPS.

3.4.4.3 Eco-indicator 95 and Eco-indicator 99

This method was developed by PRé Consultants for the Dutch government in conjunction with a large range of manufacturing companies and research agencies (Goedkoop 1995). Impacts are grouped into the categories of human health, ecosystem health and resources. The impacts are calculated based on the best available scientific knowledge. The three areas are then weighted against each other based on the distance-to-target principle.

Tool scores	
Cost	✓*
Simplicity	✓*
Effectiveness	✓✓✓

* *If materials are common and already have scores calculated, it is very cost-effective and simple. For new or less common materials, it will be more costly and less simple.*

This is one of the most widely used indicators, especially in the design area, with Eco-indicator 95 being incorporated into a range of software products and published in a simple guide to 100 common materials and processes for designers. This is a comprehensive indicator; however, like many impact models it deals poorly with land-use and biodiversity impacts. It also weighs acidification highly, which makes it a difficult model to use in the Australian situation where acidification is not a major impact.

Eco-indicator 99 (EI99) is a complete rebuild of the Eco-indicator 95 method, with substantial improvements in the modelling of damage occurring from emissions. This is done by taking greater account of the probable fate of the emission (where the emission will probably ultimately have an impact) and the sensitivity of the environment receiving that emission. It is a top-down model that begins by identifying three environmental damage end-points: human health, ecosystem quality and resources (in the same way as Eco-indicator 95). The model then analyses the damage paths from the inventory through to the predicted damage. This is done by using fate analysis to determine the sensitivity of the receiving environment (in Europe) to predict the environmental damage (Goedkoop and Spriensma 1999). The modelling approach for EI99 and fate analysis is shown in Figure 3.5.

3.5 Environmental accounting

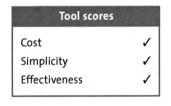

Tool scores	
Cost	✓
Simplicity	✓
Effectiveness	✓

Environmental cost accounting is a process whereby environmental costs are allocated to specific products and processes. The US Environmental Protection Agency (EPA) has developed substantial guidelines for environmental cost accounting (EPA 1995), identifying four groups of environmental costs:

- Conventional costs (direct costs)

- Hidden costs (overheads, capital and regulatory costs)

- Contingent costs (liabilities)

- Less-tangible costs (image and relationship costs)

For environmental cost accounting, costs in each of these areas listed are determined and allocated to individual products and processes. In full-cost accounting all costs (not just those relating to the environment) are allocated back to specific products and processes. This is similar to LCA; however, the flows are monetary and not physical. The aim here is to avoid cross-subsidisation of one product line through overhead and capital expenditure paid for by other product areas. It can also be used to highlight where environmental costs are being generated and how they may be reduced. Ultimately, this form of allocated costing may result in some products being discontinued as their overall costs are greater than their generated sales income.

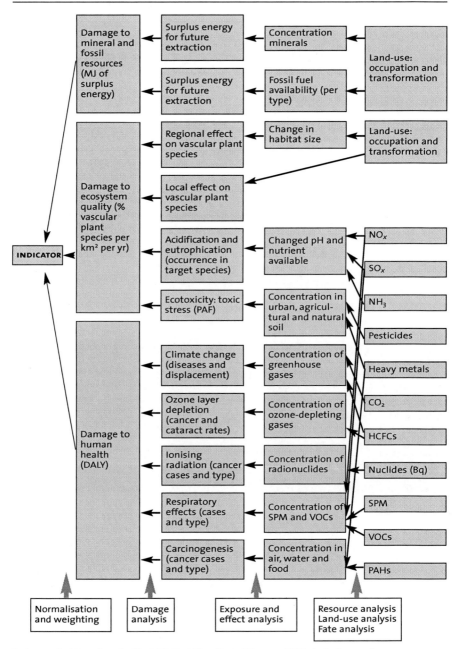

Bq, bequerels; CO_2, carbon dioxide; DALY, disability adjusted life years; HCFCs, hydrofluorocarbons; MJ, megajoules; NH_3, ammonia; NO_x, nitrogen oxides; PAF, percentage affected fraction (of species of vascular plants); PAHs, polycyclic aromatic hydrocarbons; SO_x, sulphur oxides; SPM, suspended particulate matter; VOCs, volatile organic compounds

Figure 3.5 **Eco-indicator 99 model**

Source: Goedkoop and Spriensma 1999: 11

3.6 Summary

Figure 3.6 positions the tools discussed above according to their scores and suggests areas for application. On the vertical axis is effort, which incorporates the scores of simplicity and cost; the horizontal axis is an estimate of insight, which relates to the effectiveness score. The ranking of effectiveness scores will vary by practitioners and by product and aim of assessment; however, the positioning of the tools gives some ideas on where to begin looking for an appropriate tool.

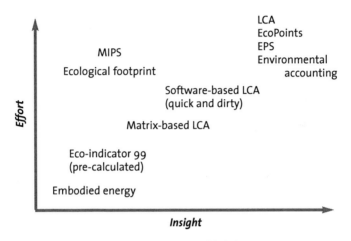

EPS, environmental priority strategies in product development; LCA, life-cycle assessment; MIPS, material input per unit of service

Figure 3.6 **Ecodesign tools matrix**

◢ Further resources

Goedkoop, M., *Life-cycle Analysis for Designers* (Eindhoven, Netherlands: European Design Centre, 1994).

> *This is an excellent introductory publication from the European Design Centre on the important role that life-cycle assessment can play in the design process. It includes case studies and illustrations to explain the fundamental principles.*

EEA (European Environment Agency), *Life Cycle Assessment (LCA): A Guide to Approaches, Experiences and Information Sources* (Environmental Issues Series No. 6; Copenhagen: EEA, http://themes.eea.eu.int/showpage.php/improvement/management?pg=40494).

> *This guide can be downloaded chapter by chapter from the Internet and gives a great overview of methods, terminology, history and information sources.*

International Journal of Life Cycle Assessment (Landsberg, Germany: Ecomed Publishers, www.ecomed.de/journals/lca/).

> *This journal provides detailed discussions and papers on LCA method and practice as well as many case studies. It also provides information on who is doing what in LCA.*

Weidema, B.P. (1998) *Environmental Assessment of Products: A Textbook on Life Cycle Assessment* (Helsinki: Finnish Association of Graduate Engineers [TEK], 3rd edn).

> *This is a well-written concise textbook of LCA covering the basic stages of LCA and issues of allocation and system boundaries. Available from TEK, Ratavaartijankatu 2, FIN-00520, Helsinki, Finland.*

◢ Useful websites

LCANET www.leidenuniv.nl/interfac/cml/lcanet/hp22.htm

> *This is a European network for strategic LCA research and development.*

ECOSITE www.ecosite.co.uk

> *This is an excellent site for looking at data, software, news and case studies on LCA.*

Australian LCA Network http://Auslcanet.rmit.edu.au

> *This site lists people and activities involved in LCA in Australia and internationally. It is also a good links page for groups working on LCA.*

ECODESIGN STRATEGIES

Ecodesign strategies are actions that can be taken to reduce environmental impacts. Ideally, strategies should be selected on the basis of an environmental assessment and a broader analysis of the product and its market. This is by necessity a pragmatic process that must address issues such as the cost of implementation (including research and development [R&D]) and the impact on retail price and sales. This chapter will focus on practical strategies for environmental improvement:

- Select low-impact materials

- Avoid toxic or hazardous materials

- Choose cleaner production processes

- Maximise energy and water efficiencies

- Design for waste minimisation

4.1 Select low-impact materials

Materials have impacts on the environment during harvesting or extraction, processing, transportation and final transformation into a product. The choice of material can also determine the durability of the product and whether or not it can be recycled.

There is no clear hierarchy of materials in terms of environmental impact, although some are better than others for any given criteria. Materials can be evaluated against many criteria, including their source (e.g. timber can be sourced from plantations or old-growth forests), method of processing, additives, energy efficiency, durability and recyclability.

Attempts have been made to compare the environmental impacts of different materials: for example, by the Tellus Institute (1992; see Table 4.1). The Tellus

Materials	Full cost (US$/ton)
Plastic	
High-density polyethylene (HDPE)	537
Low-density polyethylene (LDPE)	580
Polyethylene terephthalate (PET)	1,108
Polypropylene (PP)	602
Polystyrene (PS)	620
Polyvinyl chloride (PVC)	5,288
Paper	
Bleached kraft paperboard	443
Unbleached coated folding boxboard	382
Linerboard	394
Corrugating medium	204
Unbleached kraft paper	390
Folding boxboard from waste paper	247
Linerboard from waste paper	256
Corrugating medium from waste paper	303
Glass	
Virgin glass	157
Recycled glass	127
Aluminium	
Virgin aluminium	1,963
Recycled aluminium	342
Steel	
Virgin steel	366
Recycled steel	358

Table 4.1 **Full costs of packaging material production and disposal**

Source: Tellus Institute 1992: 46

Institute estimates the environmental costs of manufacturing and disposing of packaging materials by combining real costs (e.g. landfill disposal fees) with estimates of the price society is willing to pay to reduce the health impacts of individual pollutants.

It should be noted that comparisons based on a standard weight can be misleading because the amount of material required for the same purpose can vary significantly. The weight of aluminium required to pack 500 ml of beer is much less, for example, than the weight of glass required for the same purpose. Environmental impacts therefore need to be compared on the basis of a common functional unit, such as 'packaging for 500 ml of beer' (see Section 3.2).

As a general rule, designers should aim for four goals in material selection (Graedel and Allenby 1995: 240):

● Choose abundant, non-toxic, non-regulated materials if possible. If toxic materials are required for the manufacturing process, try to generate them on-site rather than by having them made elsewhere and shipped.

● If possible choose natural materials rather than synthetic materials.

● Design for minimum use of materials in products, processes and service.

● Try to get most of the needed materials through recycling streams rather than through raw material extraction.

4.1.1 Plastics

Plastics (or polymers) are manufactured from petrochemicals, although a new generation of polymers is being developed from starch and sugars. The first synthetic polymer, celluloid, was invented in 1870 to replace the ivory used in billiard balls. Celluloid was manufactured from cellulose from pulped cotton nitrated in acid to form nitrocellulose. Early uses of celluloid included denture plates, combs, knife and brush handles and piano keys.

Bakelite™ was invented in 1907 by reacting phenol (from coal tar) with formaldehyde (from wood alcohol). Other early plastics included nylon, polyvinyl chloride (PVC), polystyrene (PS) and polyethylene (PE). Today there are hundreds of different polymers, produced in thousands of grades for different applications.

The major stages in the manufacture of plastic products are (see also Fig. 4.1):

● Extraction of raw materials (natural gas or crude oil)

● 'Cracking' of the hydrocarbons into constituent parts, such as ethane and propane (from natural gas) or propane, butane and naphtha (from crude oil)

● Processing of the hydrocarbons into other organic chemicals, such as ethylene, propylene and benzene (the 'monomers')

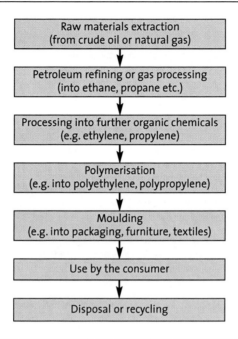

Figure 4.1 **Life-cycle of a plastic product**

● Linking of the monomers into long chains ('polymers') in a process termed 'polymerisation'

● Mixing of additives with the polymers to provide specific qualities, such as colour flexibility or colour ('compounding')

● Moulding of the polymer into a product through injection moulding, extrusion, blow-moulding and so on

The raw materials for commonly used polymers and comments on their environmental impacts are included in Table 4.2. Most plastics are manufactured from non-renewable resources such as oil and gas, and some of the intermediate products are potential carcinogens (such as vinyl chloride monomer [VCM]). Some additives are also problematic, such as lead stabilisers in PVC pipe and the plasticisers used in clingfilm. One of the main arguments in favour of plastics from an environmental point of view is their light weight, which saves energy in transport. They are also highly efficient, often requiring less material to achieve a particular function (e.g. containing a food product) compared with conventional materials.

Material	Raw material	Waste products and impacts	Energy consumption (MJ per kg)
High-density polyethylene (HDPE)	Ethylene from natural gas or crude oil	Carbon dioxide and sulphur dioxide are emitted during refining and cracking of oil to produce ethylene.	80.981
Low-density polyethylene (LDPE)	Ethylene from natural gas or crude oil	Carbon dioxide and sulphur dioxide are emitted during refining and cracking of oil to produce ethylene.	88.552
Polypropylene (PP)	Propylene gas (a by-product of oil refining)	Solid wastes include a wax by-product which can be re-used in other industries; some of the catalyst (titanium dioxide and aluminium hydroxide) goes to landfill.	80.033
Polystyrene (PS)	Benzene, a by-product of coke manufacture, and ethylene from natural gas or crude oil	Styrene monomer is a carcinogen (there are concerns for worker safety).	102.164
Polyethylene terephthalate (PET)	Ethylene glycol and terephthalic acid (from petroleum)	Steam and methanol (which is recycled)	n/a
Polyvinyl chloride (PVC)	Chlorine (from rock salt) and ethylene from natural gas or crude oil	Chlorine plants may emit mercury in water discharge; vinyl chloride monomer (VCM) is a carcinogen (giving rise to concerns for worker safety); manufacture of VCM produces chlorinated wastes.	66.805
Multi-layer plastic films	Various*	Various	n/a

n/a = not applicable

* Other polymers not listed already include ethylene vinyl alcohol (EVOH), linear low-density polyethylene (LLDPE) and polyvinylidene chloride (PVDC)

Table 4.2 **Life-cycle environmental impacts of polymers**

Sources: Boustead 1993, 1994a, 1994b

4.1.2.1 Plastics composites

Composites in common use include plastics reinforced with glass or carbon fibres. The flexibility of plastics and the strength of the fibres produce a composite with the best properties of each material. Carbon fibres are strong, heat-resistant but expensive. Glass is cheaper and relatively easy to manufacture, but there are many disadvantages. Glass fibres present a health risk to those working with them because they can be inhaled and absorbed into the body. Fibreglass is non-degradable, difficult to recycle and cannot be incinerated because the fibres are left behind in the clinker and can damage the furnace.

Research efforts are starting to focus on the use of natural fibres to reinforce plastics. Daimler Benz has been using natural fibres in its vehicles since 1995: for example, the door panels in the Mercedes G-class are made from plastics reinforced with flax fibres. The company is also investigating the use of hemp, which is more rigid and better suited to processing than flax (Hill 1997).

Biocomposites are not a new idea. In 1941 Henry Ford launched an experimental car with plastic panels attached to a tube-steel frame. The panels were moulded from hemp and ramie fibres embedded in a matrix of urea formaldehyde with wood and soybean flours. The car never reached full production (Meikle 1995: 156).

4.1.1.2 Recycled plastic

Many plastics are now available in a recycled form, including low-density polyethylene (LDPE), high-density polyethylene (HDPE), polypropylene (PP), PS and PVC. The source of the original material can have implications for the quality of the end-product. The three main sources of waste are:

- Industrial waste (i.e. manufacturing scrap, which is collected and re-used in-house)

- Post-consumer industrial waste (i.e. industrial products that have been used and discarded, such as crates, bags and film)

- Post-consumer domestic waste (i.e. packaging collected from households, such as polyethylene terephthalate [PET] and HDPE bottles)

Industrial waste tends to be relatively clean and uncontaminated. Post-consumer waste is more difficult to recycle because of the presence of contaminants such as dirt, food, paper labels and other plastics.

Recycled plastics should be used whenever possible. They are particularly suitable for applications without strict performance criteria (strength, flexibility, colour, etc.) and are often used for products

> **Design strategies for plastics**
>
> - Specify use of plastics that have less impact on the environment, such as polyethylene or polypropylene
> - Specify use of recycled plastics wherever possible
> - Use the minimum amount of material possible (lightweighting)

Plate 4.1 **Screen made from recycled high-density polyethylene (HDPE) sheet by Props Design in Melbourne. The sheet is moulded from post-consumer bottles and other HDPE scrap.**

Photo courtesy Cindy-lee Davies, Props Design

such as drainage pipes, marker posts, flower pots, bins and crates. Some recycling companies are gaining quality accreditation and can supply a product of uniform quality, which opens up a greater range of potential applications.

4.1.2 Timber

Timber is a beautiful, natural material, but harvesting can have significant impacts on the environment. The most important distinction is between timber harvested from old-growth forests and timber harvested from plantations. Regular harvesting from old-growth forests may destroy the habitats of small mammals and birds that rely on the larger, older trees for nesting hollows. Forests are being cut at an astonishing rate, destroying our natural heritage and causing long-term ecological damage. Rainforests are particularly vulnerable because of the rate at which they are being destroyed and the difficulties involved in regeneration. The United Nations Food and Agricultural Organisation (FAO) has estimated that an average of 17 million hectares of rainforest were cut down each year between 1981 and 1990 (FoE 1996). Designers should specify use of recycled or plantation timber and avoid rainforest species wherever possible.

Manufactured wood products such as medium-density fibreboard (MDF) and plywood have other environmental problems that are primarily associated with the resins and glues used in production. Formaldehyde, which is used in traditional fibreboard to bind the particles together, is classified by the Australian National Occupational Health and Safety Commission (Worksafe Australia) as a Category 2 probable human carcinogen. These are substances for which there is sufficient evidence to assume that human exposure might result in the development of cancer. Formaldehyde is a potential health risk through inhalation of particle dust in the workplace or of emissions ('off-gassing') after the product has been installed. Painting or laminating the board can reduce emissions.

Alternatives are being developed to replace MDF and plywood. An example is Gridcore™, a recycled fibre material manufactured in a honeycomb formation. The product can be manufactured from 100% recycled paper and cardboard, without resins or adhesives.

Design strategies for timber

- Specify use of plantation or recycled timber
- Avoid use of rainforest timber that has not been sustainably harvested
  - Look for labelling schemes such that of the Forest Stewardship Council [FSC]
  - Internet sites of agencies certifying timber include:
    - www.panda.org/forests4life
    - www.certifiedwood.org
    - www.ra.org
- Specify fibreboard with reduced formaldehyde content or an alternative resin binder

4.1.3 Glass

Glass was invented over 5,000 years ago and is one of the oldest packaging materials still in common use. The main raw materials are sand (to provide silica), soda ash, limestone, feldspar and recycled glass (cullet). The major stages in the manufacture of glass are (see also Fig. 4.2):

- Mining of raw materials (sand, soda ash, limestone and feldspar)
- Mixing of the materials (including the cullet)
- Melting of the materials to make molten glass
- Moulding of the glass into a product

To make glass containers, the ingredients are fed continuously into furnaces and melted at about 1,500°C. The molten glass is conveyed from the furnaces to moulding machines, where globules of glass are dropped into the moulds. Air is blown into the moulds to form bottles, which are slowly cooled.

The biggest advantage of glass is its recyclability (see Section 4.1.3.1). The environmental disadvantages of glass include the environmental impacts of mining,

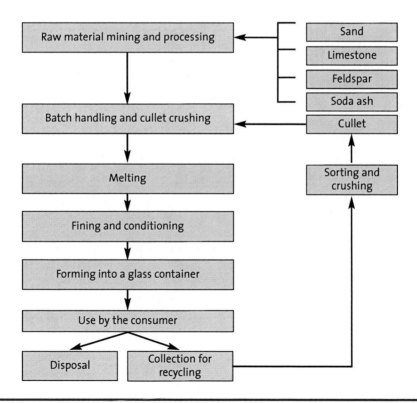

Figure 4.2 **Life-cycle of a glass container**

Source: Based on Tellus Institute 1992: §4, 2

the large amounts of energy used in manufacturing, emissions from processing and the impact of its weight on transport energy.

4.1.3.1 Recycled glass

Glass is widely recycled, and crushed recycled glass (cullet) is now the major raw material for glass manufacturing in Australia. Containers are separated into different colours (green, brown, clear) and contaminants such as metals, ceramics and plastics are removed. The glass is crushed and fed into the manufacturing process. The current recycling rate in Australia is 45%, although glass is technically 100% recyclable.

The advantages of using recycled glass are significant. The use of cullet as a raw material reduces the need for mining. Cullet also melts at a lower temperature than the raw materials and therefore does not need as much energy to be melted into molten glass. The Tellus Institute estimates that every 1% increase in use of cullet provides 0.25% in energy savings. Lower operating temperatures also reduce emissions of pollution to air (Tellus Institute 1992: §4, 9).

> **Design strategies for glass**
>
> ▪ Specify use of recycled glass
> ▪ Use the minimum amount of material required (lightweighting)

4.1.4 Aluminium

Aluminium has been manufactured only since the middle of the 19th century and its use as a packaging material is relatively recent. Aluminium is produced from bauxite ore, which is mined in open-cast mines. The ore is transported to refineries and converted into a fine white powder, called alumina, then sent to a smelting plant where the aluminium is extracted and cast into large seven-tonne ingots. Finally, the ingots are transported to fabricating plants for processing into products.

The two major additives required for alumina production are lime and caustic soda. Limestone is quarried in open-cast mines and processed to produce lime. Chlorine and caustic soda are simultaneously produced from the electrolysis of common salt (sodium chloride), which is mined from underground deposits.

Alumina is extracted from bauxite ore by means of pressure and heat (steam). Alumina is converted to aluminium through electrolytic reduction, a chemical change produced by an electric current.

4.1.4.1 Recycled aluminium

Aluminium processing consumes large amounts of energy and is therefore a major contributor to greenhouse gas generation. Like glass, however, it is easily recycled. Aluminium cans are compressed into 'bricks' and transported to processing plants. These are then fed into rotary furnaces and the aluminium is heated to

700°C. The molten aluminium is cast into ingots that are fed back into the manufacturing process.

The recycling of aluminium reduces the need for mining and processing of raw materials and for 'manufacturing' alumina and aluminium. Recycling of aluminium requires only around 5% of the energy required for virgin material, although it does add to air pollution through emissions of noxious halogens, halogen compounds and particulate matter (Tellus Institute 1992: 3-8).

> **Design strategies for aluminium**
>
> ■ Specify use of recycled aluminium
> ■ Use the minimum amount of material required (lightweighting)

4.1.5 Steel

Steel is manufactured from iron ore, coke (from coal) and recycled steel. The main steps involved in making steel are:

■ Mining and processing of iron ore

■ Limestone quarrying and lime formation

■ Mining and processing of coal

■ Coke formation from the coal

■ Sintering

■ Blast-furnace ironmaking

■ Steelmaking

■ Steel forming

> **Design strategies for steel**
>
> ■ Specify use of recycled steel
> ■ Use the minimum amount of material required (lightweighting)
> ■ Avoid mixing with different metals

There are two processes for making steel. The basic oxygen furnace process uses around 28% recycled steel, whereas the electric arc furnace process can use virtually 100% recycled steel. Coke is used in the blast furnace, where it acts as a fuel and as an oxygen-reducing agent. The production of the coke and the molten iron ('pig iron') are the stages that cause most of the pollution associated with steel production. During the coking operation around a quarter of the weight of the coal is liberated as gases and vapours, and fugitive emissions are difficult to control (Tellus Institute 1992: 26).

4.1.5.1 Recycled steel

Scrap steel from packaging, appliances, car bodies and other products is melted in a furnace to make new steel. The Steel Recycling Institute claims that, for every ton of steel recycled, 2,500 lb of iron ore, 1,400 lb of coal and 120 lb of limestone are conserved (SRI n.d.).

Post-consumer steel food and beverage cans are fully recyclable and can be manufactured back into packaging cans. The cans may need to be de-tinned to remove the fine coating of tin that covers steel food and beverage cans.

4.1.6 Paper

Paper is renewable, recyclable and biodegradable, but the production and use of paper have significant impacts on the environment. The simplified life-cycle of a paper product is shown in Figure 4.3.

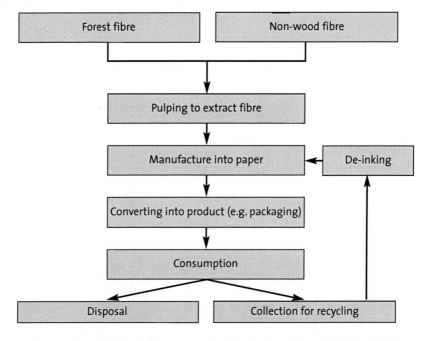

Figure 4.3 **Life-cycle of a paper product**

Most wood fibre (54%) is derived from natural regeneration forests (Table 4.3), and the global trend is towards an increasing reliance on plantations of intensively managed natural regeneration forests.

Poor forestry practices in natural forests have led to negative impacts, including loss of biodiversity, soil erosion, watershed destabilisation and reduced access for local people. Poor plantation practices have caused aesthetic uniformity and excessive water consumption. There are some positive signs, however, such as the trend away from exploitative forestry practices towards longer-term, multiple-use forest management (Greig-Gran *et al.* 1998: 55).

4.1.6.1 Non-wood fibre

Non-wood fibres can also be used for paper products and may offer environmental benefits. The 'tree-free' paper industry is growing rapidly. Such products are based on alternative fibres such kenaf, hemp, reclaimed fabric and agricultural residues.

Source	Percentage
Managed natural regeneration forests	37
Unmanaged natural regeneration forests	17
Plantations	29
Original conifer forests	15
Tropical rainforests	1
Original temperate hardwood forests	1

Table 4.3 **International sources of wood fibre**

Source: Greig-Gran *et al.* 1998: 53

Kenaf has been used in Africa, the Middle East and parts of Asia for thousands of years for clothing, rope, sacking and rugs. It also makes very good paper. Unlike southern pine, which takes 20–25 years to reach harvest stage, kenaf grows rapidly and can reach 12–18 feet in 5 months. Its fibre yield per acre is also 2–5 times higher than that of pine (Lehmer and Marden n.d.).

Hemp-based paper also offers advantages compared with conventional tree-based paper. Its yield per acre is twice that of southern pine, it competes well with weeds and is resistant to most pests. As a result, few pesticides or herbicides are required for cultivation. When modern pulping processes and mill technologies are used, fewer chemicals and less energy are required to pulp hemp fibres compared with wood fibre (Lehmer *et al.* n.d.).

Approximately 90% of all non-wood pulp is produced in Asia, much of it in small-scale mills by means of inefficient processes. The pulping of non-wood fibres uses less energy than the pulping of wood fibres, but with current technology it may be more polluting (Greig-Gran *et al.* 1998: 56).

4.1.6.2 Wood fibre

Most paper is manufactured from wood in two stages: pulping and bleaching. Pulping is used to separate the cellulose, which makes up around 75% of the wood, from lignin, resins and oils. The two major pulping processes are chemical pulping and mechanical pulping (see Table 4.4).

4.1.6.3 Bleaching

Chlorine gas and chlorine dioxide are commonly used to bleach pulp. Chlorine dioxide is considered a better environmental alternative because it produces around a sixth of the organochlorins that result from pure chlorine bleaching. This is commonly referred to as elemental chlorine-free (ECF) bleaching.

Alternatives to traditional chlorine bleaching include:

- Oxygen pre-bleaching: this removes lignin prior to chlorination, which means that less chlorine is needed.

	Chemical pulping	*Mechanical pulping*
Summary of process	Wood chips are cooked in sodium hydroxide (caustic soda) and sodium sulphide to produce strong (kraft) paper. Wood wastes are burned for fuel to run the process.	Fibres are separated by forcing debarked trees against a grinding stone of rotating metal disks.
Emissions	Hydrogen sulphide and the mercaptan family of sulphides cause a 'rotten-egg' smell. Cellulose fibres lost during the process can be discharged with waste-water, causing environmental problems. Chlorinated organics in liquid effluent, particularly dioxins and furans, are a problem in older mills.	Organic compounds have been associated with the effluent from kraft and mechanical pulp mills. Research indicates concern about their toxicity, but this is still uncertain (Greig-Gran *et al.* 1998: 57).
Advantages	It is the most efficient process for removing lignin, oils and resins. It produces high-quality pulp. It is energy-efficient.	It yields a higher percentage of usable pulp (95% compared to 45%–50% from kraft pulping).
Disadvantages	The dark colour means that considerable bleaching is required for most applications.	Product is of lower quality because lignin, oils and resins remain in the pulp, and grinding breaks the cellulose fibres. High lignin content causes the paper to darken when exposed to sunlight. It is highly energy-intensive.

Table 4.4 **Mechanical and chemical pulping of paper**

Source: based on information from 'The Paper Making Process', Canadian Magazine Producers' Association website: www.cmpa.ca/magwaste1.html

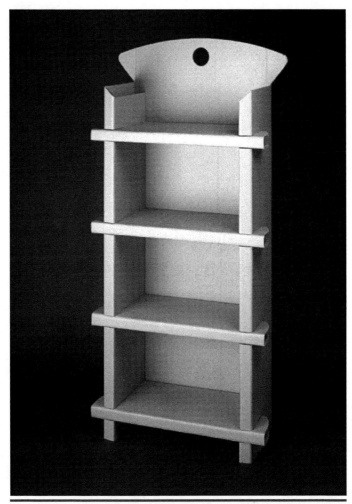

Plate 4.2 **Scrap paper and cardboard can be recycled into a wide range of products, including packaging and furniture. This bookcase has been made from recycled and recyclable corrugated cardboard, by Visy Recycling in Melbourne. The product was originally designed as temporary furniture for the Sydney 2000 Olympic Games.**

Photo courtesy Visy Recycling

- Hydrogen peroxide pre-bleaching: this converts the colour-giving parts of the lignin molecule to a colourless form, and the chemical breaks down to oxygen and water.

- Less bleaching: paper products do not always need to be white.

Papers that are not bleached with chlorine in any form are termed totally chlorine-free (TCF).

4.1.6.4 Recycled paper

Paper can be manufactured from a wide variety of waste materials, such as paper (e.g. newspapers, office paper, cardboard boxes, envelopes), textiles (e.g. cotton) and agricultural waste (e.g. sugar cane, wheat straw, rice straw). A wide variety of recycled paper grades are available for use in office paper, printing, stationery products and packaging.

> **Design strategies for paper**
>
> - Choose papers that are elemental chlorine-free (ECF) or totally chlorine-free (TCF)
> - Specify use of unbleached paper wherever possible
> - Match the brightness of the paper with its intended purpose (i.e. do not over-specify)
> - Investigate the suitability of using paper manufactured from non-wood fibres such as kenaf and hemp
> - Specify use of paper manufactured from recycled material (e.g. from waste paper and fabric offcuts)

4.2 Avoid hazardous materials

Designers should avoid specifying use of materials that are hazardous or that generate hazardous waste at any stage of their life-cycle. This includes materials that:

- Are toxic to humans or other living organisms

- Are flammable, explosive or corrosive

- Are ozone-depleting

- Contribute to global warming

4.2.1 Toxic materials

The normal definition of a toxic substance is one that, given sufficient exposure, can cause serious health effects in humans such as poisoning, respiratory problems or cancer. These include (see also Box 4.1):

- Heavy metals such as lead, mercury and cadmium

- Formaldehyde

- Chlorinated organic solvents

More detail on some of these and on other toxic substances is provided in the Appendix on pages 96-99.

Lead

- Additive in petrol
- Coating for tanks and pipes
- Glaze for ceramics
- Pigments for paints and varnishes
- Storage batteries
- Flint glass
- Stabiliser in PVC
- Electronic devices
- Cotton dyes
- Fluorescent tubes and light bulbs
- Underground cables
- Industrial paints
- Noise attenuation
- Welding or spray-coating metals
- Solder on circuit boards
- In glass for cathode ray tubes

Mercury

- Electrical devices such as lamps, rectifiers and dry-cell batteries
- Control instruments such as switches, thermometers and barometers
- Dyes (mercurachrome)
- Fungicide in wood, paints, plastics and paper
- Production of caustic and chlorine
- Fluorescent tubes
- Relays

Cadmium

- Protective coating for iron, steel and copper
- Alloys for coating other materials, welding electrodes, solders, etc.

Cadmium *(cont.)*

- Rechargeable batteries
- Stabiliser for PVC plastics (window frames)
- Pigments in paint
- Glass
- Glazes
- Electroplating, hot dipping and spraying of metals
- Deoxidiser for nickel plating
- Catalyst in plastic manufacture

Arsenic

- Manufacture of opal glass and enamels
- Textile printing
- Tanning
- Copper smelting
- Pigments
- Wood preservatives

Chromium

- Pigments
- Chrome plating
- Copper stripping
- Aluminium anodising
- Photography

Nickel

- Stainless steel
- Magnetic tapes
- Surgical and dental instruments
- Rechargeable batteries
- Electroplating
- Anodising aluminium
- Hydrogenation of fats and oils
- Manufacture of acrylic esters

PVC = polyvinyl chloride

Box 4.1 **Toxic substances and their applications** *(continued over)*

Source: adapted from Gertsakis *et al.* 1997: 34

Formaldehyde

- Urea formaldehyde and phenol formaldehyde resins used as the bonding agent in MDF, plywood and particleboard
- Urea formaldehyde insulation
- Fibreglass
- Resilient flooring
- Textiles and carpeting (crush, crease and shrink-proofing)
- Paper products
- Disinfectant and preservative in personal care products and paints

Chlorinated organic solvents

- Paint and plastic softener, paint stripper (methylene chloride)
- Resin solvent (chloroform)
- Glues (trichloroethylene)

Polychlorinated biphenyls (PCBs)

- Fluorescent lamps
- Motors
- Electric water heaters
- Large capacitors
- Transformers

Brominated flame retardants

- Printed circuit board assemblies and components
- Phenolic paper printed wiring boards
- Computer cabinets
- Kitchen appliances
- Television sets

MDF = medium-density fibreboard

Box 4.1 *(continued)*

4.2.1.1 Ozone-depleting substances

Ozone-depleting substances include:

- Refrigerants (e.g. chlorofluorocarbons [CFCs], hydrochlorofluorocarbons [HCFCs])
- Dry-cleaning agent (carbon tetrachloride)
- Blowing agents for foams (CFCs)

Alternatives exist for many ozone-depleting substances (see Table 4.5). More background information on ozone depletion is provided in Section 5.3.

4.2.2 Global warming

Global warming is the gradual increase in the Earth's temperature caused by the 'greenhouse effect'. This is produced by an accumulation of gases such as carbon dioxide, CFCs, hydrofluorocarbons (HFCs), methane and nitrogen oxides that form a 'barrier' that prevents heat loss. More background information on global warming is provided in Section 5.2.

Application	Alternatives	Comments
Aerosols	Pump packs	
Refrigeration	*Alternative refrigerants (vapour compression)*:	
	■ HFCs	HFCs are powerful greenhouse gases.
	■ Hydrocarbons, e.g. – Propane – Ethane – Butane – Isobutane	Hydrocarbons are flammable and are VOCs (which contribute to ground-level ozone pollution).
	■ Ammonia	Ammonia is toxic and flammable.
	Alternative technologies: ■ Thermoelectric cooling ■ Stirling cycle ■ Absorption cycle ■ Sonic compressor ■ Linear compressor	
Rigid polyurethane foam	*Alternative blowing agents*: ■ Cyclopentane ■ HFCs ■ Carbon dioxide ■ Pentane	HFCs are powerful greenhouse gases.
	Alternative product: ■ Vacuum panels	
Flexible polyurethane foam	*Alternative blowing agents*: ■ Methylene chloride	The volatility of methylene chloride may cause high exposure in the workplace.
	■ Carbon dioxide ■ Pentane	Pentane is flammable: safety precautions are required.
	■ Acetone	Acetone is flammable: safety precautions are required.
	Alternative products: ■ Fibrefill materials, (e.g. polyester batting)	
Extruded polystyrene and other foams	■ Carbon dioxide ■ Hydrocarbons, e.g. – Pentane – Butane – Isopentane – Isobutane	Hydrocarbons are flammable and are VOCs (which contribute to ground-level ozone pollution).
	■ HFCs	HFCs are powerful greenhouse gases.

HFCs, hydrofluorocarbons; VOCs, volatile organic compounds

Table 4.5 **Ozone-depleting substances and alternatives**

4.3 Choose cleaner production processes

Cleaner production processes are those that produce less waste, whether in terms of liquid wastes discharged to waterways, solid wastes going to landfill or gaseous wastes discharged to the air. The Victoria Environment Protection Authority (VEPA) states that cleaner production has a 'strong emphasis on prevention rather than cure'; 'it includes changing management practices, processes and product design to prevent or reduce the production of waste, rather than the traditional and outdated approach of installing "end-of-pipe" fixes to treat waste before discharge to the environment' (VEPA 1997: 56).

The product designer can play an important role in reducing manufacturing waste. By reviewing the total life-cycle impacts of a product, a designer should be able to identify any processes that are wasteful or hazardous. These need to be specifically addressed in the design brief and the subsequent design process.

Production wastes can be reduced in two ways:

- By working with production staff to select materials and/or processes that are less wasteful

- By working with purchasing staff to identify suppliers that meet 'industry best practice' in cleaner production

Many companies have achieved environmental and economic benefits by implementing cleaner production programmes. Some brief examples are provided below.

4.3.1 Footwear industry

Clarks, the largest footwear manufacturer in the United Kingdom, cut its solvent emissions by almost half between 1992 and 1996. This was achieved through a combination of initiatives, including (ENDS 1996b: 18-20):

- Switching to water-based inks for finishing uppers

- Colour moulding rather than inking soles

- Eliminating the use of solvents for brush and machine cleaning

4.3.2 Automotive industry

Ford Australia Ltd manufactures passenger vehicles. In 1992 the company implemented a cleaner production initiative designed to reduce waste from cleaning the skids used for transporting car bodies through the paint shop. The existing caustic paint-stripping process was replaced with a high-pressure water-jet system. The project resulted in annual savings of Aus$300,000 from reduced chemical, energy and waste disposal costs. Paint quality was also improved through the ability to clean skids on a more regular basis (VEPA 1997: 56).

4.3.3 Hardware industry

Gainsborough Hardware Industries in Australia manufactures door fittings such as handles, key locks and dead bolts. Components are given a range of surface finishing treatments to provide an acceptable finish and corrosion resistance. A number of electroplating processes were used in the past, culminating in a cyanide gold plating operation for some products. The waste-water from this process contained cyanide, which required special treatment. Gainsborough replaced the gold cyanide process with an electrophoretic system, which has saved the company around Aus$54,000 per year from reduced waste disposal and trade waste costs (VEPA 1997: 18-19).

4.3.4 Strategies to reduce industrial waste

Common industrial wastes are listed in Table 4.6 (for more detail on each of these waste-streams, see Graedel and Allenby 1995). Graedel and Allenby (1995) suggest a series of priority steps in auditing and minimising process residues. The first step is to determine whether any of the waste-streams contain toxic materials. If they do, it may be possible to redesign the process to substitute more benign alternatives (e.g. vegetable-derived compounds are replacing chromium in the tanning of leather). The next step is to minimise waste: for example, by re-using rinse water or eliminating leaks. A more detailed list of strategies is included in Box 4.2.

Solid waste	Liquid waste	Gaseous waste
Trace metals	Trace metals	Chlorofluorocarbons (CFCs)
Plastics	Nutrients	Hydrochlorofluorocarbons (HCFCs)
Paper	Solvents	Halons
Biological residues	Oils	Carbon dioxide
Radioactive residues	Organic compounds	Methane
Sludge	Acids	Nitrous oxide (N_2O)
Powders	Suspended solids	Volatile organic compounds (VOCs)
Mixed rubbish		Nitrogen oxides (NO_x)
		Sulphur dioxide (SO_2)
		Trace metals
		Odorants

Table 4.6 **Common industrial waste**

4.4 Maximise energy and water efficiencies

The most significant environmental impacts of a product often occur during usage as a result of the consumption of energy and other resources such as water,

- Eliminate residue streams that contain substances under phase-out regulatory restrictions, such as chlorofluorocarbons (CFCs), halons and polychlorinated biphenyls (PCBs)

- Minimise the use of de-ionised water, the generation of which consumes substantial amounts of energy and the use of which generates an additional residue stream to worry about

- Avoid the introduction or substitution of new residue streams requiring new discharge permits, modifications to existing permits, or off-site disposal

- Eliminate or minimise residue streams containing toxic substances, especially those found on regulatory lists

- Redesign factory layouts and product routings during manufacture to eliminate all unnecessary cleaning steps

- Replace processes using organic solvents with processes using water-based solvents

- Substitute less volatile chemicals for more volatile chemicals in industrial processes (e.g. produce low-volatility paints)

- Change processes to eliminate the use of volatile solvents altogether (e.g. produce solvent-free inks and coatings)

- Attempt to reduce the temperatures of manufacturing processes

- Avoid using heavy metal catalysts by substituting processes that achieve the same products by reactions between environmentally benign chemicals

Box 4.2 **Cleaner production strategies**

Source: Graedel and Allenby 1995: 225

detergents and paper. This not only depletes resources but also results in emissions to the ecosystem. These problems can be reduced by maximising the product's efficiency and by using energy sources and other resources that have minimal environmental impact.

4.4.1 Maximising efficiency

4.4.1.1 Design for energy efficiency

Reducing the energy consumed by a product results in savings to the environment, the consumer and the manufacturer. Energy-efficient products are quieter, weigh less and offer lower maintenance and other performance improvements. Manufacturing costs can be lowered through reduced material and components costs. However, for some products the market demand is for greater energy consumption where power is falsely considered to result in better performance. For example, vacuum cleaners have traditionally been sold on the wattage of the motor used rather than on a measurement of function (suction watts).

The following guidelines should be followed for energy-efficient design (Gert-sakis *et al.* 1997):

- Clarify core functions

- Look for synergies

- Aim for maximum efficiency

- Look for waste

- Design for part-load operation

- Optimise system efficiency

- Plan for ongoing efficiency improvements

- Analyse failures

- Use computer modelling to support laboratory work

Clarify the core functions
Many innovative, energy-efficient solutions fail in the marketplace because insufficient attention has been paid to the full range of functional requirements. For example, early water-efficient showers were unpopular because they did not 'feel' right, did not rinse shampoo from hair very well and left the user cold—even though they cleaned the dirt off. Energy efficiency does not replace other functional requirements: it is an additional feature.

Look for synergies
Most products are based on intermeshing systems—improving efficiency of one element often means beneficial changes in other parts. For example, improved insulation may allow the use of a smaller compressor or heating system; smoother water flow may permit smaller ducts or pipes and smaller pumps.

Aim for maximum efficiency
If you assume that a system is fairly efficient and that only minor improvements are possible by changing one or two components, you will sell yourself short. By exploring how much energy is needed to carry out a task at maximum feasible efficiency, the energy flows through the product will be better understood. Assumptions about how a product works will be more easily questioned and opportunities for savings more easily recognised. For example, an average Australian refrigerator requires only 25 kWh of electricity per annum (assuming a highly insulated cabinet and a compressor operating at theoretical limits). A five-star family refrigerator uses around 600 kWh and even the most efficient products use 200 kWh—so there is still plenty of room for improvement (Gertsakis *et al.* 1997: 37).

Look for waste
Waste often takes the following forms:

- Leaks. Heat leaks that bypass insulation can dramatically affect the efficiency of products that heat or cool; even a bolt or a bracket bridging across insulation can noticeably reduce the overall resistance to heat flow.

- Standby energy. Energy used to maintain an appliance in readiness for operation (e.g. pilot lights or electronic controls), or to run digital displays or indicator lights, can be significant; for example, the 5 W of power often required to run the digital display of a microwave oven can, over the life of the oven, exceed the amount of electricity used for cooking in the appliance.

- Cycling losses. When a system starts up or shuts down there are often transient losses as components heat up or cool down or as fluids fill or drain from the spaces; for example, household hot water pipes may hold several litres of water that must be replaced before the user receives hot water, yet this water was once heated.

- Components working against each other. Often, much of the energy used by equipment is to overcome loads created by its own components; for example, fans and lights inside refrigerated cabinets create heat loads that must be removed by the compressor system.

Design for part-load operation
Many items of equipment, such as heating and cooling systems, are optimised for operation at full load, yet this condition rarely occurs. Often, such systems are extremely inefficient at part load. Design should aim for high efficiency over the entire range of possible operational conditions.

Optimise system efficiency
If one element of a system is improved, and the mode of operation changes, savings may be compromised because of increased losses from other parts of the system. For example, if a high-efficiency ducted heating or cooling unit is developed that runs at lower output for longer periods, the longer running time means greater losses will occur through duct insulation unless that insulation is upgraded. These increased losses may exceed the efficiency gains from the improved heating or cooling unit.

Design for a range of conditions
Rarely do field conditions match those in the laboratory, and these can seriously affect system performance. For example, refrigerators in many hotel rooms and offices are built in poorly ventilated cabinets—this creates greater cooling loads and reduces compressor efficiency.

Plan for ongoing efficiency improvement
Some energy efficiency features may be too expensive, bulky or unreliable for the product being developed today. These problems are likely to be overcome over time, so they could be added in the future. The designer should keep in mind what is possible, and work on making it happen, so that the product can take advantage of, or even accelerate, developments in related areas.

Analyse failures
Designers sometimes attempt to incorporate energy efficiency features in prototypes that then fail to perform to expectations. They then reject the concepts, instead of trying to identify why it did not work the way it should. Often, preliminary designs attempt to defy simple laws of physics, or crude construction means that they cannot work properly. It pays to analyse closely why an expected improvement did not deliver savings: this process can often help to develop a better understanding of the operation of the system and lead to identification of other problems or savings opportunities.

Use computer modelling to support laboratory work
Computer modelling is often painted as complex and sophisticated, requiring substantial resources. Simple spreadsheet models, which require only a few days or weeks to develop, can facilitate identification of inefficiencies and the rapid optimisation of systems. Comparison of model results against laboratory tests allows realistic evaluation of overall system efficiency and performance. A computer model is very useful for wide-ranging 'What if?' studies.

4.4.2 Using cleaner energy sources

Using a clean energy source greatly reduces the environmental effects of energy consumption. Options to consider when selecting a clean energy source are:

- Choose the energy source with the lowest environmental impact for the location of product use. Natural gas appliances are often more efficient and result in fewer greenhouse gases than electrical appliances reliant on coal-fired power plants.

- Encourage the use of rechargeable batteries when batteries are required. This can be achieved by supplying battery chargers with the products. However, products that use either type of battery system are less efficient than mains-powered products and often use excessive standby power.

- Encourage the use of clean and renewable energy sources. Renewable sources include solar, wind and water power; cleaner energy sources are low-sulphur diesel and unleaded petrol.

4.4.3 Design for water efficiency

Many of the principles of energy efficiency also apply to water efficiency. Wherever possible, water should also be recovered and re-used. This may require filtration and cleaning mechanisms, depending on the product. The manner in which a product is used by the consumer is also important in reducing water consumption. Options to encourage water-efficient behaviour include:

- Use of default mechanism that automatically resets the appliance to its most efficient setting

- Use of feedback mechanisms on the product to show how much energy or water is being consumed

4.4.3.1 Water labels

Many eco-labels use water efficiency as part of their measurement criteria. Australia is one of the few countries that has a water rating system. Based on a rating system of A, AA and AAA (where AAA is considered the top rating), this voluntary system covers a range of products, from shower heads to white goods such as dishwashers.

4.5 Design for waste minimisation

Waste minimisation in nature is a series of cyclical systems where materials are re-used or recycled as part of a closed loop. Industry is now starting to mimic this process through 'industrial ecology', where the waste from one process or product forms the raw material for another. This ideal is still very much in the distance, however, as the complex systems to be achieved are currently only on a small scale. Industrial ecology programmes have also tended to focus on production processes, without considering consumption and post-consumption processes.

Today there is a need to design for current waste management systems that are less than perfect. Therefore it is important to take proactive measures to prevent products from entering the waste-stream, by extending the life of the product before considering other waste disposal options.

Strategies for product waste minimisation include:

- Source reduction

- Extending the product life

- Product re-use

- Product remanufacture

- Materials recycling

- Design for minimal consumption

- Minimising the impacts of disposal

These are all discussed below. More detailed strategies for particular product groups are discussed in Chapters 6–9.

4.5.1 Source reduction

Source reduction is waste prevention. This can be achieved by eliminating unnecessary components such as outer packaging that has no role in containing or protecting a product. It can also be achieved through use of lightweighting: for example, by reducing the amount of material required for a particular function. Lightweighting of packaging, such as use of PET bottles to contain soft drinks and use of aluminium rather than steel for cans, has been occurring for many years as a way of reducing costs.

Source reduction has many environmental benefits. It obviously reduces the amount of material requiring disposal at the end of the product's life. It also reduces the environmental impacts involved at almost all stages of the product's life. If a product uses less material, this means:

- Fewer resources have to be mined, extracted or harvested to make the basic materials (e.g. less bauxite for aluminium, or less oil for PET).

- Less energy is needed to process the materials.

- Fewer emissions and wastes are produced in manufacturing.

- Less energy is needed to transport the product because of the lighter weight.

> **Design strategies for source reduction**
>
> - Simplify the product: eliminate unnecessary components
> - Use the minimum amount of material required to meet performance requirements
> - Avoid unnecessary packaging
> - Use strong and lightweight materials

4.5.2 Extending product life

By designing products to last longer it is possible to reduce both resource use and waste generation. The broad concept of durability is to keep products functional, efficient and culturally relevant over a longer period than most consumers have come to expect. However, in some cases, if the complete life-cycle impact of a product is considered, durability may have an adverse effect on the environment by reducing the adoption of environmentally desirable technological innovations such as increased energy efficiency or emission controls.

The OECD, in its report, *Product Durability and Product Life Extension* (Butlin 1982), noted that a major concern resulting from product life extension is that the introduction of environmentally desirable technologies may be delayed, as in the

Plate 4.3 **These plastic sachets have achieved source reduction through sale of the product (fabric softener) as a concentrate and through use of a lightweight film package.**

Photo courtesy Packaging Council of Australia

case of pollution control devices on cars. The report recommends that it may, in some cases, be socially desirable to encourage premature replacement of durable goods that are still in working order if the environmental gain is sufficient.

Upgradability, or modular design, is a form of product life extension that is concerned with the ability of products to be upgraded as technology or styling changes. This is particularly relevant to electrical and electronic products (see Section 9.4.3).

Design strategies for extending product life

- Identify and eliminate potential weak points in the design, particularly for operational parts (methods such as failure mode and effect analysis [FMEA][1] can assist with this process)

- Ensure the product is designed for likely misuse as well for the intended use

- Design for easy maintenance and repair, preferably by the owner

- Consider classic design or other means that will encourage consumers to want to retain products for longer periods

1 FMEA is a systematic approach that identifies potential failure modes in a system, product or manufacturing operation caused by design or manufacturing process deficiencies. It also identifies critical design or process characteristics that require special controls to prevent or detect failure modes.

4.5.3 Product re-use

Re-usable products may have a lower impact on the environment than single-use products; however, life-cycle environmental impacts need to be considered in the design process to minimise any additional impacts of re-use (e.g. collection and cleaning). Examples of products that are re-used are ceramic cups, fountain pens and refillable packaging.

4.5.4 Product remanufacture

Remanufacturing is the restoration of used products, or components, to a condition that has performance characteristics that are similar to new products. It results in extension of product life and promotes the re-use of components and materials. It is therefore a means to both waste prevention and resource reduction. Remanufacturing is widely used in the areas of automotive components and industrial and commer-

---

Design strategies for re-usable crockery and packaging

- Ensure that the product is strong enough to withstand repeated collection, handling, washing and refilling

- Ensure that cleaning processes meet standards for food, beverage and personal care products

- Use in-mould labels rather than paper and plastic labels (which can be washed off or accidentally removed)

- Design packaging for a number of ways of re-use:
  - For return to the manufacturer for refilling
  - For return to the retailer for refilling
  - For re-use in the home

Plate 4.4 **These commemorative coffee canisters have been designed for re-use in the home.**

Photo courtesy Packaging Council of Australia

cial equipment; however, it is relatively uncommon in domestic products.

Although not appropriate for all situations, remanufacturing has a range of potential benefits for manufacturers and the environment. Environmentally, remanufacturing takes advantage of the original manufacturing and investment in materials and energy rather than reducing the product to its base materials. Economic benefits can also result from a reduced need to purchase new components.

One of the world's largest single remanufacturers is the US Department of Defense, which has a continuous programme of remanufacturing to maintain everything from guns to battleships. The automotive industry has the largest number of remanufacturers, providing the consumer with a practical and economical alternative to new components. For example, a factory-rebuilt starter motor is 30% cheaper than an equivalent new item (OTA 1992).

> ### Design strategies for product remanufacture
>
> Design for remanufacturing is similar to design for recyclability (see Section 4.5.5). The following principles should be followed when considering a design for possible remanufacture. The product:
>
> - Should be 'mature' (i.e. not undergoing rapid change, in terms of design or materials used); products favoured for remanufacture are those with a slow rate of design changes from year to year
> - Must be standardised and made with interchangeable parts
> - Must be capable of disassembly
> - Must have parts that can be repaired, refurbished or replaced economically to enable the final remanufactured product to reproduce the original performance
> - Must have a 'core', which must retain a sufficient value to justify remanufacture

To assist with remanufacturing, products need to be designed for disassembly so that components can easily be taken apart for repair or replacement.

4.5.5 Materials recycling

Recycling is the recovery and reprocessing of materials into a form that can be re-used in another manufacturing process.

The technologies used for recycling vary depending on the material, its source and its end-use. Some of these are described in Section 4.1. They include:

- Granulating and extruding waste plastics into recycled pellets
- Shredding and pulping waste paper
- Shredding and re-melting steel
- Crushing and re-melting glass cullet

The most traditional form of recycling is undertaken by scrap metal merchants who find it economically viable to recover metals from products such as cars and appliances. The scrap shredder was introduced into the secondary metals industry in 1961, and its growth has been rapid. Prior to the introduction of the shredder, scrap metal was compressed into bales.

Plate 4.5 **Crushed drink cans ready for recycling**
Photo courtesy EcoRecycle Victoria

The recyclability of materials depends both on technical recyclability (how easy or hard it is to recover and reprocess the material) and on practical recyclability (the availability of a infrastructure for recovery and reprocessing). Recycling of metals is well established in most countries; for example, the USA has achieved recycling rates of 56% for metal packaging and 32% for durable goods. Plastics recycling is not as well developed, with rates of 9% for packaging and 4% for durable goods (Franklin Associates 1999: 12).

Plastics tend to be more difficult to recycle, for a number of reasons:

◼ The wide range of plastics in the market, which need to be separated before recycling

◼ The high cost (poor economics) of collection and processing relative to the use of virgin polymers

◼ A loss of quality during the recycling process, which can limit potential end markets

Chemical recycling is the breakdown of plastic waste into re-usable fractions for reincarnation as polymers, monomers, fuels and chemicals. This process is developing as a possible means to recycle plastics without loss of properties. At this stage, use of the technology is fairly limited, but one day it may be suitable for separating co-mingled plastics into their original form (Leaversuch 1991: 26).

If products are manufactured from more than one material, they need to be taken apart (or 'disassembled') to separate the different materials. Cars have been among the first products to undergo thorough recycling through disassembly.

Since 1991, both BMW and Volkswagen have developed disassembly plants to recover materials such as plastics, elastomers and glass that are generally considered waste in the shredding process. In addition to developing more advanced recycling techniques, the disassembly plants offer a greater understanding of how to design cars that are easier to recycle (Redd 1992: 82-83).

Products that are manufactured primarily from steel can be shredded to recover ferrous and non-ferrous metals. The remaining material ('fluff' or 'floc') is usually disposed of to landfill or incinerator. Some success has been achieved in utilising residuals. In Australia, car batteries that are shredded for their lead content also contain polypropylene that is recycled for use in horticultural, agricultural and building and construction industries (Sims-Metal 1991: 36).

In the USA, shredder residues have been converted into structural panels. After dirt, glass, residuals metals and stones are removed, the remaining polymers are converted into a material that exhibits properties similar to masonite (PIA 1983).

The concern about plastics and other non-metals is that they downgrade the potential of materials that are becoming more common in many appliances. The recovery of these materials prior to shredding can result in recycled materials with identical properties to virgin materials.

Unlike metals, most materials can only be recovered through disassembly to keep them free from contamination and therefore to retain their original properties. Design for disassembly enables the more efficient separation of materials for optimal recycling. Design-for-disassembly principles are explained clearly in the GE Plastics publication, *Design for Recycling* (1992).

The model for complete recycling through disassembly developed by Canon in association with GE Plastics (Canon 1993: 9) involves:

- Collection of worn and obsolete appliances

- Disassembly and separation of non-compatible materials

- Sorting of different materials types

- Cleaning of components ready for re-use or recycling

Design strategies for materials recycling

Simple products

For packaging and other single-material products, the important principles are to:

- Choose materials that are commonly recycled (e.g. PET, HDPE, cardboard and metals)

- Ensure that materials used for labels, adhesives and caps are compatible with the primary material (or can be removed in the recycling process)

Disassembly and recycling

- Minimise material variety
- Use compatible materials
- Specify use of materials with recycled content
- Consolidate parts
- Reduce the number of assembly operations
- Simplify and standardise component fits and interfaces
- Identify separation points between parts
- Use water-soluble adhesives where possible
- Mark materials to enhance separation

Also:

- Before any component is re-used it needs to be quality-inspected.

- Recyclable materials are either prepared for other industry use or recycled in-house.

- Materials recycled in-house need to be quality-checked for conversion into quality-consistent material before being used in a new application.

A number of products have been developed using these principles. The most famous are a range of speculative projects developed by GE Plastics and Fitch, Richard & Smith (Wood 1992: 16-27). Such projects include a refrigerator and a kettle, which represent primarily a means of exploring the potential for plastics recycling. The kettle has been commercially released under a variety of brand names and has been criticised for not being supported by any product collection system. Therefore, although the kettle is potentially easy to recycle, it is unlikely that it ever will be.

4.5.6 Design for minimal consumption

In addition to consuming energy and water, a range of other consumables may be required for products to function: for example, detergents, coffee filters, batteries, toner and so on. All of these have a range of environmental effects, from the energy and material required to produce them to their contribution to solid waste at disposal. Wherever possible, these products should be designed for re-use, remanufacture or recycling.

Dyson vacuum cleaners are an example of a product where consumables have been avoided and where performance has been improved. It differs from other vacuum cleaners in that it is 'bag-less' (most other vacuum cleaners use 60 bags over their lifetime). The designer, James Dyson, found that bags become clogged, thus reducing suction power. Suction in the Dyson vacuum is based on a unique cyclonic system, where dust is then channelled into a collection container that is easily emptied when full. The advertising slogan for the Dyson vacuum cleaner is '100% suction 100% of the time' and seems to have been successful as the product now has over 50% market share in Britain.

Design strategies for minimal consumption

- Design the product to minimise the use of extra materials (e.g. design photocopiers and printers that offer duplexing)

- Offer feedback to consumers on when replacement consumables are required to save wastage

- Determine if consumables can be replaced by re-useable items (e.g. printer toner cartridges, vacuum cleaner filters)

4.5.7 *Minimising the impacts of disposal*

4.5.7.1 Degradability

Designing a product for degradability is useful only if the product is likely to be disposed of in a composting facility or a bioreactor landfill. Most landfills are sealed and capped to prevent degradation, which results in gas emissions and leachate.

Materials that can degrade rapidly include paper, cardboard and starch-based plastics. Glass, metals and petrochemical based plastics take many years to degrade and should be recycled or re-used rather than left to degrade.

Starch-based plastics are biodegradable under composting conditions and are currently used for bags, cutlery, plates, surgical supplies and agricultural films. They are also used for plastics that may end up in the marine environment and that may cause damage to marine life if they do not degrade.

4.5.7.2 Safe disposal

Products should be designed for safe disposal at the end of their life. Products that contain toxic materials should be labelled with instructions for decontamination and disposal. Toxic materials that could contaminate surface- or ground-water after disposal should be avoided (e.g. in inks, dyes, pigments, stabilisers, solders and adhesives).

Design strategies for minimising the impacts of disposal
■ Use degradable materials if appropriate
■ Avoid toxic materials
■ Provide instructions for proper disposal on the label

◢ Further reading

Graedel, T.E., and B.R. Allenby, *Industrial Ecology* (Englewood Cliffs, NJ: Prentice–Hall, 1995).

> *This is an excellent textbook on industrial ecology, with practical information and guidelines within a global context.*

Mackenzie, D., *Green Design: Design for the Environment* (London: Laurence King, 1991).

> *This is one of the first illustrated guides to cover environmentally oriented design across disciplines, from industrial, graphic, textile and fashion design through to architecture, landscape architecture and interior design. It takes a case-study approach with numerous colour images accompanied by simple, informative text.*

Murphy, J., *Recycling Plastics: Guidelines for Designers* (1994; Techline Industrial Data Services Ltd, 31 North Street, Carshalton SM5 2HW, UK).

> *Murphy has compiled information from a range of sources into one manual. The publication covers issues such as design for easier recycling, existing materials and technologies available for recycling, existing disposal methods and associated costs.*

Royal Melbourne Institute of Technology (RMIT), Co-operative Research Centre (CRC) for Waste Management and Pollution Control and Victoria University of Technology (VUT) Centre for Packaging, *Life Cycle Assessment for Kerbside Recycling of Domestic Paper and Packaging* (2001, http://daedalus.edc.rmit.edu.au/dfe/lcawm1.htm).

> *The report on this web page describes the results of a study undertaken to compare the impacts of recycling with those of landfill.*

◢ Useful websites

Association of Plastic Manufacturers in Europe (APME)   http://lca.apme.org

> *This site includes the results of life-cycle assessments of common plastics undertaken by Ian Boustead for APME.*

Eco-specifier   http://ecospecifier.rmit.edu.au

> *This website provides a guide to sourcing environmentally preferable materials in Australia, written by the Centre for Design at the Royal Melbourne Institute of Technology (RMIT) and the Society for Responsible Design.*

Global Recycling Network   http://grn.com

> *This website includes company directories, prices, publications and news.*

Plastics Resource   www.plasticsresource.com/recycling/index.html

> *This is a website of the American Plastics Council, giving a directory of recyclers, products and general information.*

Appendix: hazardous materials

Material	Impacts	Industries and products using the material
Antimony	Antimony is toxic.	Antimony is used in lead acid batteries, paint, alloys, semi-conductors, bullets and flameproofing compounds.
Arsenic and arsenic compounds	Arsenic is highly toxic and can be harmful through inhalation, absorption through skin and mucous membranes or through ingestion.	Arsenic is used in the manufacture of a wood preservative as copper chrome arsenate.
Asbestos	Exposure to asbestos fibres or dust can cause lung disease.	White asbestos is used within the automotive industry in brake linings and disc pads.
Barium and barium compounds	Barium salts exhibit acute and/or chronic toxic effects.	Barium compounds are used in the production of paints and pigments.
Beryllium and beryllium compounds	Beryllium and its salts are carcinogenic and cause severe respiratory distress and other toxic effects.	Beryllium is used as an alloying agent in the manufacture of springs, X-ray and electrical components and parts.
Cadmium	Cadmium is a confirmed human carcinogen and is a human poison by inhalation and possibly other routes. Cadmium accumulation in humans has been linked with hypertension and bronchitis.	Cadmium is used in alloys by the metal coating and finishing industry. Cadmium sulphide is used as a pigment in plastic. Cadmium is also used in red, yellow and maroon pigments by the paint industry.
Chromium	Most chromium compounds are toxic. Cr^{+6} is the most toxic form.	Chromium is used by many industries, including metal finishing.
Cobalt and cobalt compounds	Cobalt and cobalt compounds can be toxic, causing severe allergic reactions and irritation.	Cobalt is used in certain alloys by the automotive industry. Cobalt can be used as a catalyst by the chemical industry.
Cyanides (inorganic)	Most inorganic cyanides are poisonous even at low concentrations.	Inorganic cyanides are used by the metal-finishing industry.

Material	Impacts	Industries and products using the material
Halogenated organic solvents*	Halogenated organic solvents may result in immediate or delayed adverse impact to the environment by means of bioaccumulation and/or toxic effects. Many are human carcinogens by inhalation. Some solvents can effect the environment by depleting the ozone layer.	Halogenated solvents are used by industry because of their ability to dissolve a wide range of organic contaminants, their low flammability and their high vapour pressure.
Inorganic fluorine compounds (excluding calcium fluoride)	Metal fluorides are very toxic.	Fluorine is used in high-temperature plastics and toothpaste.
Isocyanate compounds	Inorganic isocyanates are only slightly toxic, but organic cyanates can cause irritation and allergic reactions in the eyes and in the gastro-intestinal and respiratory tracts.	Isocyanates are used in the production of polyurethane, paints, building insulation materials and in the automotive industry.
Lead and lead compounds	Lead may result in adverse impacts on the environment by means of bioaccumulation and/or toxic effects.	Lead is used in the manufacture of pigments for paint, polyvinyl chloride (PVC) plastic, batteries and many other products.
Mercury and mercury compounds	Mercury vapour is toxic. Mercury can be converted into a dangerous form by bacteria present in rivers, lakes and seas. Mercury may result in adverse impacts on the environment by means of bioaccumulation and/or toxic effects.	Mercury is used in electrical appliances (lamps, mercury arc reflectors), control instruments (thermometers, barometers) and dental amalgams.
Metal carbonyls	Some carbonyls are extremely toxic.	Carbonyls are used in the synthesis of tuolene diisocyanate, which is an intermediate in the manufacture of polyurethane plastic.

* Halogens include fluorine and chlorine.

Material	Impacts	Industries and products using the material
Nickel compounds	Nickel and many of its compounds are poisons. All airborne nickel-containing dusts are regarded as carcinogenic by inhalation.	Nickel is used in the manufacture of stainless steel, rechargeable batteries, magnetic tapes and many other products.
Non-halogenated organic chemicals	Most non-halogenated organic chemicals are toxic.	Non-halogenated organic chemicals are used in the chemical (polymer) industry and consist of polyol, derivatives of polyol, formaldehyde and acrylamide.
Organic solvents	Most solvents are flammable and toxic. Some solvents are petrochemically reactive.	Non-halogenated solvents such as xylene, toluene ketones and mineral turpentine predominantly arise from the paint industry.
Oxidising agents including chlorates, perchlorates, peroxides	These substances cause or contribute to combustive processes by yielding oxygen on reaction, and may explode on heating.	Hydrogen peroxide is used as a bleaching agent by the paper recycling industry.
Phenols and phenol compounds	Phenol is flammable, corrosive, mutagenic and acutely toxic, with the potential to cause immediate collapse or death.	Phenol is used as a starting chemical for manufacturing phenolic-derived polymers. Phenolic compounds are used in disinfectants, deodorisers, paints and as a binding agent.
Phosphorus and phosphorus compounds	Phosphorus is a very poisonous and highly flammable substance, causing severe burns to the skin, other irritating effects and is potentially fatal.	Phosphorus is used in the manufacture of bronze, steel, pesticides, matches and special glass.
Selenium and selenium compounds	Selenium fumes are poisonous causing irritation of the nose, throat and lungs.	Selenium is used in photocopying processes (photocopier drum). It is also used by the electronic and glass industries.
Silver and silver compounds	Silver is poisonous.	Silver thiosulphate is used in photographic film processing.

Material	Impacts	Industries and products using the material
Tellurium and tellurium compounds	All tellurium compounds are highly toxic. Tellurium is a rare metal.	Tellurium is used for alloying with cast iron and stainless steel. It is used by the electronics industry in the production of semiconductors.
Thallium and thallium compounds	Thallium and thallium compounds have extreme neurotoxic effects with a delayed response to exposure.	Thallium is used in the electrical and electronic industries.
Polychlorinated biphenyls (PCBs)	PCBs are carcinogenic.	PCBs originate in transformers and power capacitators (lamp ballast).
Zinc compounds	Zinc-bearing wastes are considered to be hazardous.	Zinc is used in large amounts in alloys such as a brass and galvanising. Zinc oxide is used in a wide range of products in the rubber industry, and as a white pigment in paint. The main producer of zinc waste is the plastic industry.

Source: VEPA 1998: 67-80

THE ECOLOGY
OF PRODUCTS

5.1 The ecological footprint

Every product we make and use contributes to environmental degradation in many different ways. It has an 'ecological footprint' that extends well beyond national boundaries and long after a product has been used and discarded. There are many tools available to help the designer assess the environmental impacts of a product, including life-cycle assessment (LCA) and eco-indicators. These are discussed in Chapter 3. The aim of this chapter is to introduce some of the major environmental problems and their links to product design. These problems are:

- Global warming
- Ozone depletion
- Reduced biodiversity
- Resource depletion
- Water pollution
- Air pollution
- Land degradation
- Solid waste
- Acidification

The importance placed on these environmental impacts varies between countries. Acidification, for example, is regarded as a bigger problem in Europe than it is in Australia, where land degradation issues such as deforestation and salinity are having a much greater impact.

The manufacture, use and disposal of each product contributes to environmental damage in a variety of ways. This is illustrated in Figure 5.1, which shows some of the links between a refrigerator and the environment.

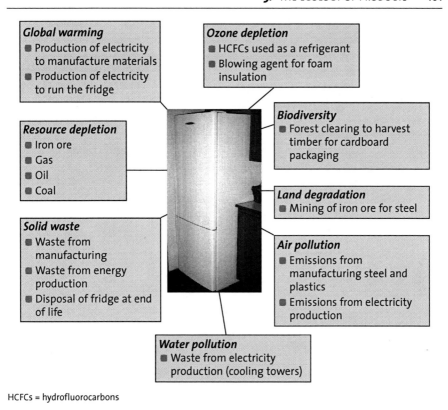

Global warming
- Production of electricity to manufacture materials
- Production of electricity to run the fridge

Ozone depletion
- HCFCs used as a refrigerant
- Blowing agent for foam insulation

Resource depletion
- Iron ore
- Gas
- Oil
- Coal

Biodiversity
- Forest clearing to harvest timber for cardboard packaging

Land degradation
- Mining of iron ore for steel

Solid waste
- Waste from manufacturing
- Waste from energy production
- Disposal of fridge at end of life

Air pollution
- Emissions from manufacturing steel and plastics
- Emissions from electricity production

Water pollution
- Waste from electricity production (cooling towers)

HCFCs = hydrofluorocarbons

Figure 5.1 **Environmental impacts of a refrigerator**

It is important to remember that, when evaluating the environmental impacts of a product or design feature, every impact needs to be multiplied by the number of units manufactured or currently in use. A single appliance may have a negligible impact on the environment, but a million appliances do not. Similarly, a small design improvement may seem trivial until the environmental benefits are calculated and multiplied by the number of units in production.

5.2 Global warming

Evidence suggests the temperature of the Earth is gradually increasing as a result of the enhanced 'greenhouse effect'. The greenhouse effect is caused naturally by the accumulation of carbon dioxide (CO_2) and water vapour in the upper atmosphere, which insulates the Earth and prevents heat loss. This effect appears to be accelerating as a result of emissions of CO_2, methane, chlorofluorocarbons (CFCs) and nitrogen oxides (NO_x) arising from human activity. The likely impacts of an increase in global temperatures include rising sea levels and increasing rain and snowfall.

An international agreement to reduce global warming, known as the Kyoto Protocol, was signed in Japan in late 1997. Under this agreement most developed countries are committed to reducing their greenhouse gas emissions to 1990 levels and then to reduce them a further 5% by 2012. Australia and Norway will be allowed to increase their emissions on 1990 levels, but with a significant reduction on previous rates of growth.

One of the major sources of greenhouse gas emissions is the burning of fossil fuels such as coal, oil and gas to produce energy. Greenhouse impacts are therefore particularly relevant to appliances that consume energy during their life, such as water and space heaters, stoves and refrigerators. The choice of fuel is particularly important, with large differences in greenhouse gas generation between alternatives such as gas and electricity (see Fig. 5.2).

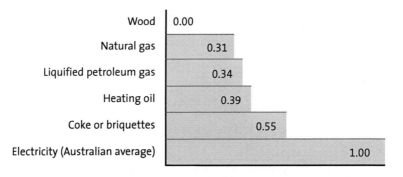

Note: It is assumed that fuel burns at 70% efficiency; transport of wood, and land clearing for timber harvesting, generate greenhouse gas emissions not included here.

Figure 5.2 **Kilograms of greenhouse gas generated per unit of heat delivered**

Source: Pears 1997: 20

Design can also have a significant impact on greenhouse gas emissions related to a single product; for example, Figure 5.3 shows the variation in greenhouse gas emissions from a variety of appliances used to boil water for hot drinks. If we all shifted to use the most energy-efficient products currently on the market, domestic energy consumption could be reduced by around 75% (Aplin *et al.* 1999).

5.3 Ozone depletion

Ozone is a form of oxygen (O_3) that forms a layer in the atmosphere between 20 km and 50 km above the surface of the Earth. The ozone layer protects us

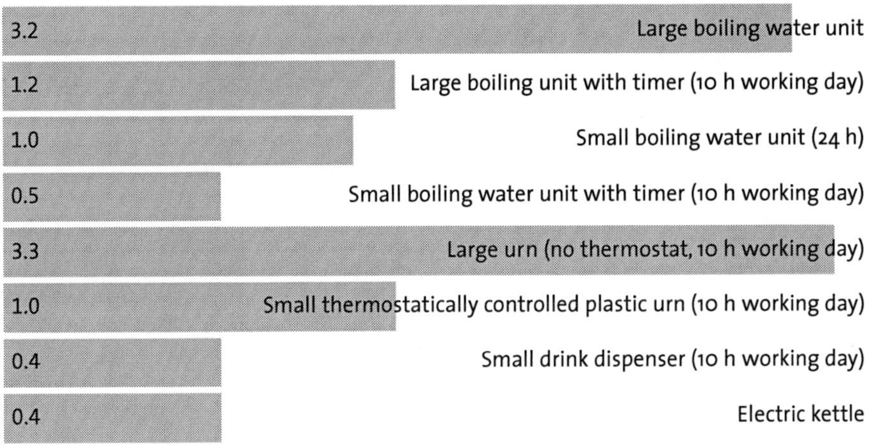

3.2	Large boiling water unit
1.2	Large boiling unit with timer (10 h working day)
1.0	Small boiling water unit (24 h)
0.5	Small boiling water unit with timer (10 h working day)
3.3	Large urn (no thermostat, 10 h working day)
1.0	Small thermostatically controlled plastic urn (10 h working day)
0.4	Small drink dispenser (10 h working day)
0.4	Electric kettle

Figure 5.3 **Annual greenhouse gas emissions of ways of supplying hot water for drinks (tonnes carbon dioxide per year, 60 cups per working day for a year)**

Source: Sustainable Solutions 1993

against the harmful effects of the sun's radiation. Ozone is destroyed by reaction with nitric acid (created by the burning of fossil fuels) or chlorine compounds (e.g. CFCs used in refrigeration or foams).

Ozone-depleting substances are being phased out under an international agreement called the Montreal Protocol (see Table 5.1). These chemicals have traditionally been used as propellants, refrigerants and blowing agents. Recent evidence suggests that bromine-based chemicals are also damaging the ozone layer, but are not covered by the Protocol (Aplin *et al.* 1999).

5.4 Reduced biodiversity

Biodiversity is reduced when the number of plant and animal species is reduced at a local, regional or global level. This can occur for a number of reasons, for example:

- Land clearing for urban development, mining or other human activities

- Timber harvesting or clear-felling in old growth forests

- Pollution of air, soils or waterways

Tropical rainforests are among the most biologically diverse habitats (e.g. they are home to at least half the world's plant species). They are also experiencing extreme rates of species extinction (Aplin *et al.* 1999).

Ozone-depleting substances	Developed countries	Developing countries
Chlorofluorocarbons (CFCs)	Phased out end of 1995	Total phase-out by 2010
Halons	Phased out end of 1993	Total phase-out by 2010
Carbon tetrachloride	Phased out end of 1995	Total phase-out by 2010
Methyl chloroform	Phased out end of 1995	Total phase-out by 2015
Hydrochlorofluorocarbons (HCFCs)	Freeze from beginning of 1996 35% reduction by 2004 65% reduction by 2010 90% reduction by 2015 Total phase-out by 2020	Freeze in 2016 at 2015 base level Total phase-out by 2040
Hydrobromofluorocarbons (HBFCs)	Phased out end of 1995	Phased out end of 1995
Methyl bromide	Freeze in 1995 at 1991 base level 25% reduction by 2001 50% reduction by 2005 Total phase-out by 2010	Freeze in 2002 at average 1995–98 base level

Table 5.1 **Summary of Montreal Protocol control measures**

Source: CEPA 1996

Scientists and policy-makers are still grappling with complex issues relating to how we measure and protect biodiversity in the environment. Designers need to be aware that any product made or derived from biological resources, such as timber, may have implications for biodiversity. Impacts can be minimised through careful selection of materials (e.g. timber certified by the Forest Stewardship Council [FSC]), design for material efficiency and use of recycled materials and by-products.

5.5 Resource depletion

Many of the raw materials we use are non-renewable, and supplies are limited. In 1972 a report to the Club of Rome warned of dire consequences to humankind unless exponential growth in population and consumption could be controlled:

> If the present growth trends in world population, industrialisation, pollution, food production, and resource depletion continue unchanged, the limits to growth on this planet will be reached sometime within the next one hundred years. The most probable results will be a rather sudden and uncontrollable decline in both population and industrial capacity (Meadows et al. 1972: 23).

On a positive note, we are starting to see a change in the relationship between industrial growth and consumption of energy and raw materials. The World Commission on Environment and Development (WCED 1987) noted that, while growth has continued in developed market economies, the demand for many basic raw materials has levelled off or declined. Energy consumption per unit of gross domestic product (GDP) in countries in the Organisation for Economic Co-operation and Development (OECD) has been dropping at a rate of 1%–3% every year since the late 1960s. Between 1973 and 1983, energy efficiency improved in OECD countries by 1.7% annually.

This is a positive trend, but there is no room for complacency. World population is increasing at a rate of almost 100 million people per year and is expected to reach 10,000 million by 2050. Developing countries account for 95% of the increase, but every additional citizen in the USA adds statistically more stress to the natural environment than 20 citizens in India or Bangladesh (von Weizsäcker *et al.* 1997).

Resource conservation should be considered in the design, manufacture, use and disposal of every product. Materials need to be used efficiently and recovered at the end of their life for recycling. In their book, *Factor Four: Doubling Wealth, Halving Resource Use*, Ernst von Weizsäcker, Amory Lovins and Hunter Lovins argue that we can use resources at least four times more efficiently than we do now, without compromising our quality of life, and the authors provide numerous examples to support their claim (von Weizsäcker *et al.* 1997).

5.6 Water pollution

The most common sources of water pollution are discharges from industrial processes, household sewerage, storm-water drains and run-off from agriculture. Waterborne wastes from industrial processes may include trace metals, nutrients, solvents, oils, organic substances, acids and suspended solids (see Table 5.2).

Water pollution can have a visual impact, but it can also be hazardous or toxic to aquatic life. Suspended solids in water reduce water clarity, and turbid waters are poor habitats for fish and other aquatic life. Trace metals can be toxic to aquatic life and can bioaccumulate in the food chain.

Industries contributing to waterborne emissions of trace metals include electroplating, leather tanning, the use of heavy metals in printing inks (although this is declining significantly as alternatives become available) and the use of batteries with high concentrations of heavy metals. Solvents are widely used in industry to remove scale, rust and other surface contaminants from metals.

Water pollution is also generated during the use of some appliances (e.g. detergents in waste-water from washing machines and dishwashers). These impacts can be minimised through use of biodegradable detergents or through better design of the appliance to minimise water use.

Process	Trace metals	Nutrients	Solvents, oils	Organic substances	Acids	Suspended solids
Agriculture	n/a	●●●	n/a	●●●	n/a	●●●
Chemical manufacture	●●	n/a	●	●	n/a	●●
Electronics	n/a	n/a	●	●●	n/a	n/a
Electroplating	●●●	n/a	●	n/a	n/a	●●
Fertiliser	n/a	●	n/a	n/a	n/a	●●
Food production	n/a	●●	n/a	n/a	n/a	n/a
Leather making	●●	n/a	n/a	●	n/a	n/a
Metal cleaning	n/a	n/a	●	●	n/a	●
Mining, smelting	n/a	n/a	n/a	n/a	●	●●●
Pesticides, herbicides	n/a	n/a	n/a	n/a	●	n/a

●   Modest impact on local, regional or global scale
●●   Minor influence on local, regional or global scale
●●● Major influence on local, regional or global scale
n/a   Not applicable

Table 5.2 **Waterborne wastes emitted by common industrial processes and products**

Source: Graedel and Allenby 1995: 212

When products are disposed of to landfill they can generate water pollution by leaching metals or other toxic substances into ground-water.

5.7 Air pollution

Sources of air pollution include emissions from factories, power-generating plants, wood fires and motor vehicles. Typical pollutants include CO_2, NO_x, sulphur dioxide (SO_2), ozone and volatile organic compounds (VOCs). The environmental impacts of air pollution include:

▓ Global warming (e.g. by CO_2, methane)

▓ Ozone depletion (e.g. by CFCs)

▓ Acid rain (e.g. from SO_2)

▓ Health impacts (e.g. from solid particles)

Air pollution has reduced significantly in many developed countries following the introduction of environmental regulations, emission controls and lead-free petrol. Since the mid-1980s the number of 'smog alert' days in Melbourne has dropped from about 100 per year to between 15 and 20. In many Australian cities, smoke from wood heaters and open fires has overtaken motor vehicles as the major source of particle air pollution, which can cause a range of lung diseases in winter. Pollution from diesel engines is also a cause for concern because of the growing number of diesel-powered small commercial and four-wheel-drive vehicles (Strong 1998: 15).

Design can play a major role in reducing air emissions from vehicles. Between 1973 and 1986 the average car made in the USA became twice as efficient, from needing 17.8 litres fuel per 100 km to needing 8.7 litres fuel per 100 km. About 4% of the savings came from making cars smaller, and 96% from making them lighter and better (von Weizsäcker *et al.* 1997: 4-5). Increasing efficiency means less fuel is burned, resulting in lower air emissions. 'Ultralite' concept cars manufactured with strong, lightweight composite materials and a hybrid-electric drive instead of the conventional engine have the potential to reduce fuel use by 80%–95% and to cut 90%–99% of air emissions (von Weizsäcker *et al.* 1997: 10).

5.8 Land degradation

Land degradation concerns the adverse effects that various uses of land by humans have had on the environment. These effects include reduced soil fertility, soil erosion, salinity of land and water, weed invasion, removal of topsoil and deforestation.

The 'ecological footprint' of many products involves mining to generate energy and to extract mineral ores. This can require the movement of enormous quantities of soil and rock ('overburden') to get access to minerals, and large amounts of ore need to be crushed and processed to extract valuable metals. A gold ring weighing 10 g, for example, requires the mining and processing of 3 tonnes of ore (von Weizsäcker *et al.* 1997: 242).

Open-cast mining involves the removal of vegetation and causes disruption to local ecosystems. For this reason metals should always be used efficiently and recycled. Each tonne of recycled metal used in manufacturing eliminates the need to extract thousands of tonnes of ore.

5.9 Solid waste

Despite recent initiatives to expand recycling programmes and encourage source reduction, the amount of waste we throw away is still increasing. Between 1960 and 1997 the amount of waste thrown away per person in the USA increased by 45%. During the same period, materials recovery increased from 6.4% to 28% of total waste, but this was insufficient to counteract the increase in waste generation. The increase in waste generation has been attributed to increased economic activity and consumption levels (Franklin Associates 1999: 3-5).

Products generate solid waste in manufacture, use and disposal. Some of this waste is recycled, but most is disposed of in incinerators or landfills. Incinerators generate air pollution and toxic ash (which must also go to landfill), and landfills generate methane gas and waterborne pollutants that can pollute ground-water. Many of these pollutants can be traced back to everyday products (e.g. heavy metals in printing inks and old paint tins, lead oxide in television tubes and light bulbs, and cadmium in rechargeable batteries). Landfills also take up valuable land that could otherwise be used for urban development, agriculture or other higher-value uses.

It is no longer acceptable to manufacture products for single use (e.g. disposable packaging) or to design 'durable' appliances with in-built obsolescence. When products are thrown 'away', they do not just disappear—they sit in holes in the ground for hundreds or thousands of years.

Archaeological 'digs' in landfills have revealed the fact that biodegradation in modern landfills is very slow or non-existent. Well-known US 'garbologist' Dr William Rathje claims that, although some degradation of organic material does occur, 'well-designed and managed landfills seem to be far more apt to preserve their contents for posterity than to transform them into humus or mulch' (Rathje 1992: 112). He points out that:

> Biodegradation works most efficiently under composting conditions, when debris is chopped up, regularly turned, kept wet and exposed to the oxygen that microorganisms, which biodegrade organic material in the most straightforward way, require. These conditions are not met in modern landfills. The garbage stays where it has been dumped, tightly compacted but largely intact (Rathje 1992: 117).

The implication for product designers is that choosing a biodegradable material such as paper or a starch-based plastic will not automatically eliminate waste. Unless the product is likely to end up in a compost facility or a bio-reactor landfill, it is still likely to remain intact in the ground for tens or hundreds of years.

The most common materials found in municipal waste (by weight) are paper and paperboard, organic materials such as garden trimmings and food, and plastics (see Table 5.3).

5.10 Acidification

'Acid rain' is caused mainly by sulphur dioxide, nitrogen oxides and other pollutants that are released into the atmosphere when fossil fuels such as oil or coal, which contain sulphur, are burned. Acid rain can be carried many kilometres in air currents before falling to the ground, which explains why Scandinavia receives acid rain from factories in Germany, and why Canada receives acid rain from factories in the USA. Acid rain kills wildlife and trees (Collins 1995: 3).

Once again, the imperative for the designer is to choose cleaner sources of energy (such as gas or solar energy) and to design for maximum efficiency.

Material	Percentage of total municipal waste (by weight)
Paper and paperboard	38.6
Yard trimmings	12.8
Food	10.1
Plastics	9.9
Metals	7.7
Glass	5.5
Rubber, leather, textiles	6.8
Wood	5.3
Other	3.3
Total	100.0

Table 5.3 **Composition of domestic waste in the USA, 1997**

Source: Franklin Associates 1999: 9

◢ Useful websites

World Resources Institute (WRI)   **www.wri.org**

> The WRI claims to 'provide information, ideas and solutions to global environ-mental problems'. It publishes annual reports on the state of the environment (e.g. WRI 1998) and has an excellent website.

United Nations Environment Programme (UNEP)   **www.unep.org/SGE/**

> This website provides a summary of UNEP's first report on the global environment (UNEP 1997) as well as links to national and regional reports on the state of the environment.

6

PACKAGING

Packaging has probably received more attention in the environmental debate than any other manufactured product. This is because packaging is one of the most visible components of the waste-stream, making up around one-third of the average household's rubbish (LRRA 1996) and over half of all items in the litter stream (Industry Commission 1996). As a result of this attention, packaging has been one of the most interesting fields in which designers have had the opportunity to demonstration their ability to design for the environment.

Packaging is designed to contain, protect and promote a product. The volume of packaging has increased exponentially over the past 40 years, owing to rapid growth in the population, a shift to convenience products, self-serve retailing and the development of new materials and new methods of food preservation. These trends have resulted in a dramatic increase in the amount of waste generated by packaging.

Most packaging is designed for disposal after single use. This is highly wasteful of resources and energy and is unsustainable in the long term. It also contributes to the growing volume of solid waste that must be either recycled or, more commonly, sent to landfill for disposal. Waste disposal practices have improved dramatically since the days of the unregulated rubbish tip, but even modern landfills have environmental risks associated with them. Leachate from landfills can include heavy metals and other toxic materials, which have the potential to contaminate ground-water and surface-water. Degradation of organic material produces methane, which contributes to global warming.

Pressure is being applied to the packaging industry through the introduction of government regulations in Europe, the USA, Japan and other countries around the world. The first and most significant product stewardship legislation was introduced in Germany in 1994. The Directive on Packaging and Packaging Waste (1994) required industry either to accept all returned packaging or to provide for its collection and recycling. Industry created the Duales System Deutschland (DSD), a system to recover packaging separately from general rubbish collection. Through the DSD, a 'green dot' trademark is licensed to companies in return for a fee based on the type and quantity of packaging used. The DSD system has led to a dramatic increase in recycling rates for packaging and to the redesign of packaging to eliminate unnecessary components.

Other European countries such as Austria, France and Belgium have since adopted similar legislation. The European Parliament adopted the European Union (EU) Directive on Packaging and Packaging Waste in December 1994, establishing a framework for management and recycling of packaging materials. This framework includes five-year packaging recovery and recycling goals for member states and sets specific requirements for packaging waste reduction within member states. All members of the EU are required to comply with the Directive.

In Australia, the voluntary National Packaging Covenant was signed by governments and industry in 1999, with backup legislation being passed progressively by state governments to regulate 'freeloaders' (Packaging Council of Australia n.d.). In Japan, the Law for Recycling of Containers and Packaging (1995) has been enforced for glass, plastics and paper packaging (Raymond Communications 2000). These are indicative of the types of policy being introduced to control packaging waste and are going to have a significant impact on product design in the future.

From an ecodesign perspective, the aim of the packaging designer should be to minimise waste by avoiding unnecessary packaging, reducing material use and designing for re-use, recycling or degradability. The designer can also minimise environmental impacts by carefully selecting materials and by avoiding use of metal-based inks.

6.1 Selecting materials

The choice of materials for a package has implications for the environment at every stage of the product life-cycle. These need to be carefully evaluated in the context of the design brief to ensure that the best material is selected. This means weighing up environmental impacts, functional requirements (transport, retail display and use), market acceptability, cost and manufacturing issues.

Traditional packaging materials such as wood, clay, banana leaves and raffia may be a source of inspiration for ecodesigners but are unlikely to be suitable for mass production in a modern industrialised economy. Japan appears to be fairly unique among developed countries in its ability to use natural materials such as straw, clam shells, bamboo grass and timber for exquisite packaging (Taschen 1993).

More common packaging materials include metals (aluminium and steel), paper, cardboard, glass, plastics and composites. There is no material currently in use that is ideal from an environmental perspective because each material has advantages and disadvantages. Boyden *et al.* (1991) found that it is not possible to rank one container system ahead of another on environmental grounds. This is because each system (e.g. glass, liquid paperboard, high-density polyethylene

[HDPE]) performs differently depending on which environmental indicator is used (i.e. energy, mineral use, greenhouse gas production, generation of air or water pollutants or production of solid wastes).

This was also the conclusion of a major study of packaging, undertaken by the Tellus Institute (1992), a non-profit research organisation in Boston, MA. The aim of the study was to investigate whether the problem with packaging is simply its sheer volume in landfill or whether some forms of packaging are worse for the environment than others. Researchers undertook a detailed life-cycle analysis of glass, aluminium, steel, five types of paper and six types of plastic. For each material they compared air and water pollution from the manufacturing process, monetary costs of waste management, and air and water from the waste management process.

Some of the conclusions of the study have important implications for packaging designers:

● Recycled materials. In every case where data was available for recycled and virgin materials, production of recycled materials was found to have lower impacts on the environment than virgin materials. Therefore, recycled materials should be used wherever possible.

● Polyvinyl chloride (PVC). PVC was found to be the material with the worst impact on the environment because it causes emissions of vinyl chloride monomer and other carcinogenic substances during production. Although PVC is difficult to replace in some applications, all of the packaging uses of PVC could be replaced by other, less damaging materials. The Tellus Institute found that switching form PVC to other materials would be the most important step in reducing toxicity of packaging.

● Waste reduction. The study compared the environmental impacts of each package, and, apart from PVC, found that the lightest-weight packages were almost always the least harmful for the environment. This highlights one of the most significant design strategies for reducing environmental impacts—source reduction. This is discussed in more detail in the next section.

6.2 Source reduction

A variety of strategies can be used to minimise packaging waste. These include:

● Avoiding unnecessary components
● Lightweighting
● Design for re-use
● Design for recycling
● Design for degradability

6.2.1 Avoiding unnecessary components

One of the criticisms constantly directed at the packaging industry is that many products are 'over-packaged'. Opportunities to reduce packaging depend on the specific needs of the product for containment, protection, transport and marketing. Three types of packaging have been defined (Saphire 1994: 3):

● Primary or consumer packaging, which is the basic package containing the product and is kept while the product is consumed (e.g. a soft-drink bottle, a toothpaste tube or a flour bag)

● Secondary packaging, which is additional packaging used to facilitate self-service sales, prevent theft or further advertise and market the product and tends to be thrown away after the product is opened (e.g. a toothpaste box or six-pack drink carrier)

● Transport or distribution packaging, which is used to ship goods from their point of origin, such as a factory or farm, to their destination (e.g. a cardboard box, a pallet, shrink-wrap, strapping and polystyrene beads)

Most opportunities to eliminate components are in the secondary packaging category. Toothpaste boxes have been virtually eliminated in countries with strict waste laws such as Germany. The tube itself has been redesigned in many cases to allow for the change, for example by switching from aluminium to plastic to minimise damage in transit and by making the lid larger so that the tube can stand up on a flat surface. The need for additional display packaging, such as a notched plastic tray, may have reduced the overall waste reduction benefits, however.

In countries with less regulation, such as the USA and Australia, there are numerous examples of packaging on supermarket shelves that is not essential to contain or protect the product. Flour is sold in simple paper bags, but in some cases the same paper bag is packed inside a cardboard box. This type of secondary packaging can easily be eliminated. Men's shirts are another classic example— folded around cardboard, held together with pins, packed in a strong plastic box and given to the customer in a plastic shopping bag.

Transport packaging is less likely to be excessive, but opportunities exist to reduce waste and save money through a more careful assessment of packaging needs. Stretch wrap can be eliminated, for example, by using a spray-on resin to secure unitised loads without the need for further packaging. The product is a hydrogen-bonding polymer applied in liquid spray form, which locks the boxes together in a horizontal direction. The bond can be broken easily by lifting the boxes vertically. The polymer does not damage the boxes or leave any residue. Pittsburgh Brewing found that switching from stretch wrap to the resin saved them US$27,000 per year—US$9,000 in stretch wrap and US$18,000 in overtime pay because of the ability to load pallets faster (*Packaging Digest*, June 1994).

Plate 6.1 **Stretch tape manufactured by 3M is used to stabilise loads on pallets. By replacing stretch wrap it reduces waste by around 95%.**

Photo courtesy 3M and Safetech

6.2.2 Lightweighting

Like all products, packaging has environmental impacts at every stage of its life-cycle. Production of a plastic milk bottle, for example, requires extraction of natural gas, cracking in a refinery, polymerisation into HDPE, blow-moulding into a bottle, filling, transportation to the supermarket and the home, disposal or recycling (see Fig. 6.1). Although most attention has focused on waste disposal, every stage of the life-cycle consumes resources and energy and produces waste. The most effective way of reducing these impacts is to produce less packaging in the first place (i.e. for reduction at source).

A study by the Centre for Design at the Royal Melbourne Institute of Technology (RMIT) found that the selection of material and the design of a package

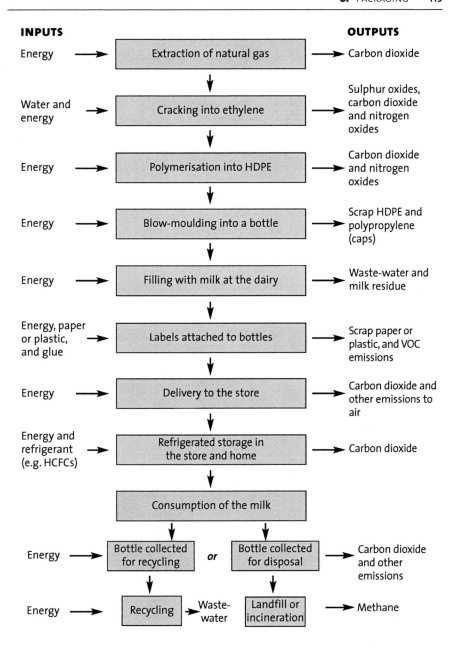

HCFC, hydrofluorocarbon; VOC, volatile organic compound

Figure 6.1 **Process tree for a high-density polyethylene (HDPE) milk bottle**

can have a greater impact than the recycling rate on the amount of waste disposed to landfill (Grant and Lewis 1997a). The study compared the 'efficiency' of almost a hundred packages by determining the amount of material thrown away at the end of the product's life. All packages were standardised for a given amount of product: for example, all milk packaging was expressed as the amount of packaging material per litre of milk. An allowance was made for recycling rates or recycled content by deducting the higher of the two: for example, the weight of a glass bottle package was reduced by the relevant recycling rate (43%).

The results of the study clearly show that lightweight packages produce less waste than packages manufactured from materials with higher recycling rates. The example shown in Table 6.1 for milk packaging is indicative of the results for other products. The most efficient form of packaging for milk, in terms of material discarded per litre of milk, was found to be the plastic bag (glass packaging was not analysed because milk is not commonly packaged in glass in Australia). The results for milk also illustrate some of the options for increasing efficiency through source reduction; for example:

- Packaging in bulk (4 l rather than 2 l bottles)

- Choosing a lightweight material (plastic rather than liquid paperboard)

- Choosing a flexible package (a bag rather than a bottle)

- Concentrating the product (powdered rather than fresh milk)

Product	Package type	Material	Recycling rate (%)	Packaging discarded per litre of milk (g)
Fresh milk	Plastic bag	LDPE	0	6.2
Fresh milk	4 l bottle	HDPE	42	10.9
Fresh milk	2 l bottle	HDPE	42	12.3
Fresh milk	2 l gable-top carton	Liquid paperboard	12	27.7
Fresh milk	1 l gable-top carton	Liquid paperboard	12	27.9
Fresh milk	500 ml gable-top carton	Liquid paperboard	12	30.8
Powdered milk	1 kg bag	Laminated plastic	0	2.9

LDPE, low-density polyethylene; HDPE, high-density polyethylene

Table 6.1 **Waste from milk packaging**

Source: Grant and Lewis 1997a: 69

Plate 6.2 **One of Colgate Palmolive's laundry detergents, sold in the Enviropack pouch and a refillable high-density polyethylene (HDPE) bottle**

SMITHKLINE BEECHAM DEVELOPS, MANUFACTURES AND MARKETS pharmaceuticals, vaccines, over-the-counter medicines and health-related consumer products. The company has a product stewardship policy that aims to consider environmental and safety issues at every stage of a product's life-cycle. It is a signatory to the International Chamber of Commerce (ICC) Business Charter for Sustainable Development.

SmithKline Beecham has made extensive use of life-cycle assessment to assist in understanding the environmental benefits of source reduction. In 1994 in North America the company launched a new toothbrush pack. The new design was a lightweight polyethylene terephthalate (PET) blister pack, which replaced a rigid polystyrene box wrapped in cellophane. The new pack uses 70% less material and, with 16 million units sold annually, the company claims to have saved 160 tonnes of plastic, 6,000 tonnes of air emissions and 116 million MJ of energy (ENDS 1996b).

Instant Horlicks™ has also been improved to pack more efficiently, resulting in an overall reduction in packaging of 15 tonnes per year. For example, the 500 g pack has been reduced in height by 7%. In addition to direct packaging savings, the change also enables pallets to hold an extra layer of packs, resulting in 13% fewer truck journeys

Box 6.1 **Case study: SmithKline Beecham packaging**

Source: SmithKline Beecham Environment and Safety Report 1998
(www.sb.com/company/esr/1998/04stew.htm)

Multi-layered plastic films are allowing source reduction through greater use of bags and pouches. Colgate Palmolive has introduced a refill pack system, using a stand-up pouch (Plate 6.2), for its laundry detergents and fabric softeners. The pouches are manufactured from a multi-layered film, with a flat bottom to allow them to stand up on a flat surface. They weigh around one-quarter of the weight of their plastic-bottle equivalent.

Coussins uses a lightweight HDPE plastic refill bottle for its Radiant laundry liquids, which are also sold in larger, durable PVC bottles. The refill packs are recyclable and, more importantly, weigh 75% less than the original bottle. This represents a significant saving in raw materials and in the environmental impacts of production. Within four months of its introduction, the refill accounted for 45% of product sales (Grant and Lewis 1997a: 32).

Packaging in bulk is another way of increasing the product–package ratio and thereby improving efficiency. Bulk soap and shampoo dispensers in hotel rooms, for example, are a major improvement on the thousands of small bottles that are thrown away each year in a large hotel.

6.2.3 Design for re-use

Re-usable packaging is not as common as it was 20 years ago, but it is starting to show signs of a resurgence in use. The generally accepted 'waste hierarchy' places re-use above recycling because the product is not thrown away after single use. Comparisons of single-use and re-usable products based on an assessment of total life-cycle impacts show that such rules of thumb do not always apply, however. Re-usable bottles tend to be heavier than single-use bottles, which means that they consume more raw materials in manufacture and more energy in transport. The washing process requires hot water (and therefore energy) as well as detergents to ensure that health standards are met.

A study by the Fraunhöfer Institute in Munich compared the environmental impacts of refillable and single-use containers for beer and milk. The study found that the 'energy break-even point' for milk delivery occurs between 18–25 trips per bottle, and between 100–200 km of travel. More trips or shorter distances mean that refillable containers are better; less trips or longer distances mean that single-use containers are better (cited in Ackerman 1997: 116).

This does not mean that re-use strategies should be avoided, but it does mean that re-use systems need to be carefully designed to ensure that environmental impacts are minimised. Schemes that encourage consumers to bring bottles back for refilling must ensure that this is done as part of a regular shopping trip rather than by adding to the energy and greenhouse impacts of transport.

The Body Shop offers a refill service for some products in most stores, including shampoos, moisturisers and other liquid skin-care products. In Australia approximately 2% of sales are through refills. This is estimated to save around 60,000 bottles or 1.3 million tonnes of material per year (Grant and Lewis 1997a: 41).

Refillable bottles for beverages and personal care products are the exception rather than the rule. Refillable bottles and drums are becoming more common in

Plate 6.3 **This innovative packaging for a refrigerator has replaced expanded polystyrene (EPS) foam, strapping and a cardboard box with re-usable foam strips and shrink-wrap. The refrigerator is manufactured by Email Ltd.**

Photo courtesy Packaging Council of Australia

the chemical industry, however, because the containers are usually contaminated after use and are difficult to dispose of in an environmentally responsible way.

Transport packaging offers many opportunities for re-use. Corrugated boxes are used in staggering numbers to transport products around the country and across the world. In the USA, approximately 25 billion corrugated boxes were produced in 1990, accounting for 12.2% of the national municipal waste-stream (Saphire 1994: 1). Corrugated cardboard is potentially recyclable, but recycling also consumes resources and energy.

Re-usable transport packaging can produce economic and environmental benefits. One study compared the amount of material used per million shipments, and found that a re-usable plastic box generates 98.5% less waste than single-use corrugated boxes (Saphire 1994: 5), although the calculation made no allowance for recycling. The results are shown in Table 6.2.

Companies often save money when they switch from disposable to re-usable boxes. Xerox Corporation in the USA has replaced thousands of different-sized one-way shipping containers with a system that relies on nine standard re-usable corrugated boxes. The new system saves Xerox around US$2–5 million annually, through (Saphire 1994: 12-13):

■ Reduced freight costs as a result of more efficient packing in shipping containers

■ Reduced product damage

Box material	Number of times used	Number of boxes used for 1 million shipments	Weight of box (lb)	Total weight of box material used per million shipments (tons)
One-way corrugated	1	1,000	1.5	750
One-way corrugated	2	500	1.5	375
Re-usable corrugated	5	200	2.2	220
Re-usable plastic	250	4	5.5	11

Table 6.2 **Comparison of material used for a million shipments in one-way and re-usable boxes**

Source: Saphire 1994: 5

■ Reduced disposal costs for one-way boxes

■ Reduced packaging costs

■ Reduced labour costs through the use of a uniform barcode system for materials tracking and receiving

■ Reduced storage costs from a smaller packaging inventory and a reduction in warehouse space

According to Sapphire (1994), re-usable containers work well under certain conditions—when there are short distribution distances, frequent deliveries, a small number of parties involved and company-owned or dedicated distribution vehicles. The containers can be made from a variety of materials (e.g. cardboard, plastic, wood, steel and fibreboard) and can be designed with features that facilitate shipping, handling and storage. These include (Saphire 1994: 7-8):

■ Collapsibility: the walls of the container are designed to fold down when collapsed.

■ Nestability: empty containers can be placed inside one another.

■ Stackability: tops and bottoms are designed to lock into one another to allow for greater stacking height.

A list of benefits of re-usable transport packaging is provided in Table 6.3.

6.2.4 Design for recycling

Design for recycling guidelines are included in the checklist in Box 6.5 (pages 127-28). These guidelines include choosing a material that can be economically recy-

Benefits to the supplier	Benefits to the receiver
Lower packaging costs (a break-even point needs to be identified)	Reduced labour costs with better-designed packaging (usually more substantial that supplier's savings)
Reduced product damage (re-usable containers are much more durable)	Handling of empty containers eliminated
Possible reduced transport or material handling costs with higher-stacking containers	No handling, packing or storage of non-returnable packaging
Elimination of fibre dust (product can be packed in production area in plastic containers)	No fibre dust in production areas
Improved warehouse utilisation (re-usable containers stack higher than single-use cartons)	Improved warehouse utilisation
Packaging tape cost eliminated	Injuries from knives used to open cartons eliminated

Table 6.3 **Benefits of re-usable transport packaging**

Source: Jones 1997: 3

cled, using only one material and ensuring that adhesives are soluble. Specific guidelines for plastic bottle recycling were developed by local councils and the packaging industry in the USA (see Box 6.2; for a case study of a company recycling plastic bottles, see Box 6.3).

Most packaging that is made from a single material is technically recyclable (e.g. PET, glass and aluminium), which means that the technology required to recycle them is known and well-established. A package is only truly recyclable, however, when a system for collection and recycling is available to most customers.

Glass, paper, cardboard, aluminium, steel, PET and HDPE are recycled at high rates in many countries. Other plastics such as polystyrene (PS), polypropylene (PP), expanded polystyrene (EPS) and low-density polyethylene (LDPE) are technically recyclable, but recycling is difficult for a number of reasons—for example, because of the:

- Small volume in the domestic waste-stream (which makes them uneconomic to collect and sort)

- High levels of contamination, particularly in food packaging (e.g. with butter, cottage cheese, yoghurt, meat)

Multi-layered films are very difficult to recycle because of the range of materials used. Films used to package meat can include up to ten layers, including layers of LDPE, linear low-density polyethylene (LLDPE), ethylene vinyl acetate (EVA), polyvinylidene chloride (PVDC) and ethylene vinyl alcohol (EVOH).

A UNIQUE DESIGN-FOR-RECYCLING PROJECT WAS UNDERTAKEN IN THE USA IN 1994 with funding from the Environment Protection Agency. The aim of the project was to reach consensus on the design changes for plastic bottles that would improve the economics of recycling. Participants included the cities of Dallas, TX, Jacksonville, FL, Milwaukee, WI, New York, San Diego, CA, and Seattle, WA. The project team also included representatives from Avery Denison, Enviro-Plastic, Johnson Controls, Owen Illinois, Procter & Gamble, SC Johnson Wax and St Jude Polymer.

The project came up with the following recommendations:

- Caps, closures and spouts on high-density polyethylene (HDPE) bottles (except 'living-hinge' applications) should be compatible so that the post-consumer resin can be marketed into high-value end uses without the need to remove caps manually.

- Aluminium seals on plastic bottles are not to be preferred unless the seal pulls off completely by the consumer.

- Caps on natural HDPE bottles should not be pigmented; where needed, coloured labels should be used for product differentiation instead of pigmenting the cap.

- Aluminium caps should be phased out on plastic bottles.

- HDPE base cups should be phased out on polyethylene terephthalate (PET) bottles.

- Adhesives on labels, including those on refrigerated bottles, should be water-dispersible during processing.

- Metallised labels should not be used on plastic bottles with specific densities greater than 1.0.

- Printing should not be directly applied on unpigmented packaging containers, except for date coding.

- Polyvinyl chloride (PVC) and polyvinylidene chloride (PVDC) film labels should be used on PVC containers only.

- All layers in multi-layered plastic bottles should be sufficiently compatible so that the post-consumer resin can be sold into high-value end-markets.

- PVC should not be used in bottles for products that are also made in resins that look like PVC (note: this recommendation was made by city participants only; industry participants thought it was inappropriate to comment and abstained).

- Manufacturers of processing equipment should pursue the development of a low-volume, low-cost, automated sorting system for detecting PVC that is practical for use in a materials recovery facility.

Box 6.2 **Design for recycling plastic bottles**

Source: Anderson *et al.* 1995: 64-65.

COCA-COLA AMATIL (CCA) HAS BUILT A recycling plant in Australia to recycle polyethylene terephthalate (PET) bottles back into food-grade resin for new soft-drink bottles (below). The process involves friction washing and decontamination to produce clean, high-quality recyclate. The reprocessed resin is used to manufacture 390 ml, 600 ml and 1.25 l bottles with 25% recycled content.

CCA has assisted in the development of a recycling guide to improve the recyclability of PET containers. The publication includes guidelines on appropriate labels, adhesives, inks, tamper-proof seals and closures.

Box 6.3 **Case study: Coca-Cola Amatil recycled polyethylene terephthalate (PET) soft-drink bottles**

Source: Beverage Industry Environment Council 2000.

All plastic packaging should be clearly marked with a polymer identification code. The most commonly used system for packaging was developed by the Society of the Plastics Industry (SPI) in the USA, and later endorsed by industry associations in Canada, Japan, Australia and Europe. The SPI code uses the numbers 1 to 7 in a recycling symbol (Box 6.4). A more detailed identification coding system has been developed by the International Organisation for Standardisation.

Liquid paperboard containers are manufactured with layers of different materials, which can make them difficult to recycle. The simplest of these is the milk carton, which is manufactured from liquid paperboard coated with LDPE. Aseptic cartons are more complicated, with up to six layers of liquid paperboard, LDPE and aluminium foil. In some countries both types of carton are recycled, primarily to extract the high-quality white fibre.

Packaging should include recycled material wherever possible. Most of the common materials can include a percentage of recycled material, particularly paper, cardboard, glass, steel, aluminium, PET and HDPE. Health regulations restrict the use of recycled material in direct contact with food, but in some cases this can be overcome through strict quality control of raw materials or use of multi-layer technology. Some plastic bottles are moulded with a layer of recycled material sandwiched between two layers of virgin material to avoid direct contact.

6.2.5 Design for degradability

Degradability is an environmental advantage if the package is likely to end up in the litter stream (e.g. plastic straws or hamburger shells) or if it can be collected

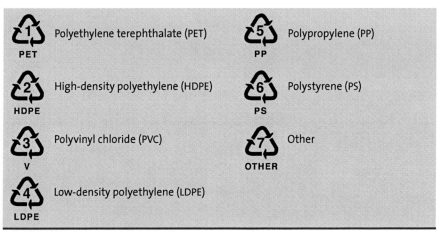

Box 6.4 **Polymer identification codes**

with other organic material for composting. Modern landfills are carefully sealed and compacted, which means that the air, water and microorganisms required for composting are rarely present. A study by well-known 'garbologist' Dr Bill Rathje found carrots and newspapers still intact after 20 years in a landfill (Rathje 1992).

Composting of organic material such as food and garden waste is becoming more common. When composting facilities become more readily available, potential applications for degradable packaging from paper, cardboard and starch-based plastics will increase. An ideal use for degradable materials would be for fast-food packaging that can be collected in special bins in restaurants and taken to a composting facility with food wastes from the kitchen.

Photodegradable polymers (i.e. those that are designed to degrade in sunlight) should be avoided unless a clear environmental benefit can be demonstrated, because most of these are manufactured from a synthetic polymer with a degradable additive. The synthetic component will break down into microscopic pieces that are invisible to the human eye, but will remain in the environment for many years. Photodegradable plastic is used for six-pack beverage can rings to ensure that the rings break and are not a risk to wildlife. This is an appropriate use of the polymer, but a completely biodegradable polymer might be an even better option.

6.3 Looking to the future

Packaging designers of the future will need to pay much greater attention to environmental performance. This will be driven primarily by regulation, particularly in Europe. Non-European countries can no longer be complacent either,

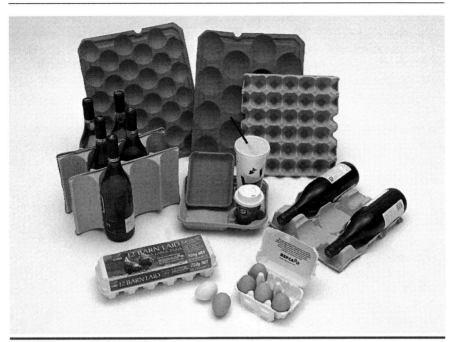

Plate 6.4 **Packaging manufactured from post-consumer recycled paper by Huhtamaki. These are manufactured with a high percentage of post-consumer recycled paper, and can themselves be recycled.**

Photo courtesy Huhtamaki

Plate 6.5 **This ice cream pack has been designed to be 100% recyclable, with the base, lid and label all made from polypropylene. Previously, the lid was made from low-density polyethylene (LDPE) and the label from paper. This new design reduces contamination in the recycling process, and improves economies of scale by increasing the total quantity of polypropylene in the recycling stream.**

since regulation of packaging in some form is being considered in most developed countries.

The key issue for packaging, in the eyes of both the regulator and the consumer, is waste. This means that designers need to consider options for waste reduction such as lightweighting and increasing the recycled content and recyclability.

At a system-wide level, manufacturers need to understand the existing recycling infrastructure. For example, if the aim is to produce a beverage bottle that can be recycled through a kerbside recycling system, the designer will need to gain a good understanding of which materials are collected and how they are reprocessed. This will have implications for the choice of primary material as well as for components such as caps and labels.

Designers also need to consider how current trends are likely to impact on waste and recyclability. Increasing consumption of pre-prepared meals, takeaway food and single-serve packs all lead to more packaging. Advances in material technologies, such as new multi-layer films to increase shelf-life, also have implications for recyclability. This may not be a bad thing, as lightweighting has been shown to have greater benefits for the environment than recycling. Nevertheless, consumers and regulators will continue to demand recyclability.

The aim of packaging designers should be to design efficient, lightweight packs that save materials and energy. As far as possible, packages should also be designed for recovery through conventional processes. In the longer term, more advanced technologies will be developed to recover a wider range of materials, particularly plastics.

A checklist for packaging design is provided in Box 6.5, and an example of a design specification for packaging and foodware materials is given in Box 6.6.

◢ Further reading

Evans, P., *The Complete Guide to Eco-Friendly Design* (Cincinnati, OH: North Light Books, 1997).

> *This is an excellent guide to minimising environmental impacts in graphic design and printing. It includes packaging case studies.*

Hewlett-Packard, *Guideline for Environmentally Responsible Packaging*, http://packaging.hp.com/enviro/environm.htm, 1994–99.

> *This was developed by Hewlett-Packard to assist its packaging professionals and suppliers to develop sound packaging and distribution strategies. It covers reduction, re-use and recovery strategies, labelling and detailed design guidelines for paper and plastics.*

Sound Resource Management Group, *Prevent Packaging Waste: A Practical Guide for Cost Savings and Environmental Benefits of Re-evaluating Business Packaging* (report to Snohomish County Public Works, Everett, WA, 1995).

> *This is a report on a project to assist businesses in reducing business packaging. It includes guidelines and case studies.*

Source reduction

- Use the minimum amount of material required to contain, protect and deliver the contents safely to the consumer
- Minimise the weight of the package
- Reduce package wall thickness
- Package products in a concentrated form
- Package products in bulk
- Keep the number of packaging layers to a minimum

Re-use

- Use durable materials to protect against damage during washing and handling
- Use in-mould labels rather that paper or plastic labels (which can wash off)
- Establish an efficient return system that takes advantage of existing networks (e.g. backloading transport packaging in delivery trucks) and returns packages to agents or retailers close to the end-user rather than to the manufacturer
- Use incentives, such as monetary deposits for containers, to encourage correct participation in re-use systems
- Use lightweight refill packs to enable re-use of bottles within the home
- Consider lending packages to the consumer rather than selling them

Recycling

- Use only one material, or materials that are compatible in recycling
- Remember that, although a material might be physically recyclable, it cannot be called recyclable if there is no infrastructure or market in place to process it
- Avoid non-recyclable laminates or multi-material films
- Minimise the number of different materials used
- Use materials that can be recycled economically
- Use materials for which there is an existing collection and recycling system
- If a collection system does not exist, assess the feasibility of collection through the kerbside system, reverse vending machines and collections in stores, schools and by community groups
- Avoid using labels, adhesives, coatings and finishes that may contaminate recycling
- Use water-soluble adhesives for labels
- Use in-mould labels or labels made from the same material
- Use integral (moulded-in) finishes rather than paint or coatings
- Ensure that inks are compatible with recycling
- Use in-mould identification symbols for plastic resins (in conformity with ISO 11469 [ISO 2000])
- Ensure that the consumer is clear about the product's recyclability

Box 6.5 **Packaging design checklist** *(continued over)*

Source: Based on Grant and Lewis 1997a: 52-54

Use of recycled materials

- Use materials from post-consumer domestic or industrial waste
- Avoid direct contact between recycled plastics and food unless approved by the relevant health authorities

Degradable polymers

- Only use degradable polymers where appropriate
- Use biodegradable polymers for products that are likely to end up in an organic (compostable) waste-stream
- Avoid photodegradable polymers unless there is a clear environmental benefit (e.g. preventing entrapment of animals in six-pack rings)

Safe disposal

- Include an anti-litter message on the package
- Minimise the incidence of toxic waste through careful selection of components
- Avoid use of inks, dyes, pigments, adhesives and stabilisers wherever possible: for example, by using in-mould labels
- Design the package to be easily compressed prior to disposal to minimise its volume in landfill
- Label packages containing toxic materials with instructions for safe disposal

Marketing

- Provide clear instructions for re-use, recycling or disposal on the label
- Avoid misleading claims

Box 6.5 *(continued)*

PACKAGING WAS STRICTLY CONTROLLED FOR THE 2000 OLYMPIC GAMES IN Sydney, Australia. Specifications were developed to control materials used for all packaging and foodware, based on the following principles.

- The responsibility for minimising packaging and foodware waste will be shared by all who are involved in its generation, use and disposal, extending from the product manufacturer, packaging manufacturers, through to the buyer and waste contractor. Successful waste minimisation will be brought about through proper implementation of the three Rs (reduce, re-use, recycle). SOCOG [Sydney Organising Committee for the Olympic Games]'s priority will be to ensure its operations and those of its contractors and service providers:

  - First, **reduce** the need for and avoid particular types and quantities of packaging and foodware waste. Contractors and suppliers will be asked to assess and advise how their products can be packaged differently to reduce waste while still maintaining product quality. Where agreed ,such measures will be implemented by contractors and suppliers.

  - Second, **re-use** packaging that is durable, re-usable and refillable and foodware products that can be used many times, without any reprocessing or remanufacturing. Examples of re-usable items include pallets, ceramic crockery and stainless steel cutlery.

  - Third, **recycle** by ensuring packaging and foodware materials are chosen because of their capability to be reprocessed, the existence of local markets for the resultant materials and that they are adequately labelled and sorted accordingly to support recycling within Olympic precincts and venues.

- **A biodegradable stream** of material that can be processed in a biowaste or compost facility has the potential to greatly reduce waste normally destined for landfill.

- Controls placed on the type and quantity of packaging material entering venues is an important first step to manage the waste-stream, reduce contamination and reduce operating costs.

Restricted materials included polystyrene, aluminium foil, disposable plastic foodware, shrink-wrap used for transport packaging, cling-wrap, composite materials and glass (for use in public areas).

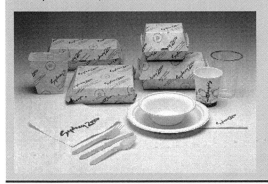

Packaging used for the Sydney 2000 Olympic Games, manufactured from recyclable and recycled cardboard, recyclable PET and biodegradable plastic

Photo courtesy Visy Industries

Box 6.6 **Case study: specification for packaging and foodware materials at the Sydney Olympics**

For further information, see Environment Australia's website at www.ea.gov.au, or Greenpeace at www.greenpeace.org.au/campaigns

7

TEXTILES AND CLOTHING

The environmental impacts of textiles are now being considered by a small but growing number of textile manufacturers, designers and specifiers. Most of the attention is focused on the impacts associated with growing or manufacturing fibre and with dyeing and finishing processes. In the clothing industry, some designers are trying to address the impact of constantly changing fashion on consumption and production.

When it comes to textiles, many people confuse 'natural' with 'environmentally friendly', assuming that natural fibres such as cotton and wool are superior to synthetic fibres. This is far from the truth. Cotton farming relies on chemicals that pollute the environment and deplete soils. Wool processing uses detergents and solvents to clean the raw wool and uses toxic chemicals in dyeing and finishing.

Synthetic fibres are not perfect, either. These are manufactured from petrochemicals that have impacts associated with oil and gas extraction, refining and processing. They also require more energy to produce than natural fibres.

The textile industry as a whole consumes large amounts of water and produces equally large amounts of polluted waste-water.

To understand the environmental impact of textiles we need to examine their complete life-cycle, which includes growing and processing the fibre, manufacturing the yarn, manufacturing the fabric, dyeing and finishing, cutting and making the final product, maintaining the product during use and disposal or recycling.

7.1 Growing and processing fibres

7.1.1 Natural fibres

Natural fibres come either from plant or from animal sources (see Table 7.1). Although these fibres are 'sustainable' in one sense—they are natural and renewable—the farming and manufacturing industries associated with them are less so.

Natural plant fibres	Natural animal fibres	Half-synthetic plant fibres	Synthetic fibres from oil or gas
Cotton	Wool	Viscose (rayon)	Polyester
Kapok	Mohair	Cupro	Polyamide
Flax (linen)	Silk	Acetate	Acrylic
Jute		Triacetate	Moacryl
Ramie		Lyocell	Arimide
Abaca			Polypropylene
Sisal			Polyethylene
Coconut			Polyvinyl chloride
Hemp			(PVC)
			Polyurethane

Table 7.1 **Sources of textile fibre**

7.1.1.1 Cotton

The cotton-growing industry is a major consumer of synthetic fertilisers and pesticides. In 1994 nearly 50 million lb of insecticides, herbicides, dessicants, miticides and growth regulators were used on US cotton. Around 10% of the world's pesticides, and 25% of the world's insecticides, are used on cotton. According to the Sustainable Cotton Project (SCP), based in California, about one-third of a pound of chemicals is used to make one T-shirt (Marquardt n.d.).

Some pesticides are toxic to humans, being linked to skin irritations, headaches, breathing problems and cancers. Aerial spraying means that the chemicals are widely dispersed in the environment.

Interest in organic cotton is growing as a result of initiatives such as the Cleaner Cotton Campaign, undertaken in 1998 by the SCP. This was an outreach programme to educate clothing manufacturers about the problems arising form chemical-intensive cotton farming. The campaign included presentations to manufacturers of sportswear, mass merchandise, apparel and textiles, by SCP founder Will Allen and fashion designer Lynda Grose (Lynda Grose was also involved in Esprit's successful Ecollection; see Box 7.3 on page 142). Organic cotton is also being promoted through the efforts of other individuals, such as Dorothy Myers from the UK Pesticides Trust, which provides funding for organic cotton projects in developing countries.

Demand for organic cotton fluctuated in the early 1990s, first increasing in response to an emerging 'eco-fashion' trend, and then declining as apparel companies withdrew from the market because of supply problems, higher costs, consumer price resistance and marketing barriers. New developments and strategies in the apparel industry are now stimulating renewed demand for organic cotton, which in 1998/99 was at an all-time high. New developments include a shift by companies to blending small percentages of organic cotton into conventional cotton products. Blending supports organic farmers without adding significantly to costs (FCPAN 1999: viii-ix).

Patagonia is an industry leader in the use of 100% organic cotton (see Box 7.1). As mentioned above, other manufacturers have chosen to blend organic and conventionally grown cotton in their products. Nike blended 3% organic cotton into more than 20 million T-shirts in 1998, and Levi-Strauss purchased 330,000 lb of organic cotton for their 501™ jeans.[1]

Australian company Maud N Lil designs and manufactures clothing from organic cotton, but the development process has been a long and difficult one. Although the organic fibre was available from a grower in Queensland, the biggest problem was finding a spinner willing to work in accordance with the important but stringent standards of the Biological Farmers of Australia. These standards require the complete cleaning of all equipment to prevent contamination of the organic product with the traditional, chemically grown product.

From early beginnings manufacturing T-shirts for Greenpeace and Australian Geographic, Maud N Lil has grown to a small but successful manufacturer of toys and clothing (Plate 7.1). The quality of the organic cotton is equal to the traditional product, and many customers prefer it because of their sensitivity to fabrics manufactured with chemicals (Epton 1997: 6).

The organic cotton market is growing rapidly. In the USA over 150 stores stock organic cotton products, including Esprit, The Gap and Patagonia. Glant Environmental Fabrics manufactures 100% organically grown cotton fabrics. The fabrics are made in Texas, from cotton grown on farms certified as organic by the Texas

Plate 7.1 **A selection of Maud N Lil toys made from organic cotton**

---

1   See The Organic Cotton Site at www.sustainablecotton.org/news001.html.

Making clothes out of conventional cotton is something our company can no longer afford to do (Yvon Chouinard, cited in Patagonia 1995: 1).

PATAGONIA IS A MANUFACTURER OF EQUIPMENT AND CLOTHING FOR OUTDOOR sports. In 1994 the company decided to convert all of its cotton clothing to organically grown cotton and began a comprehensive research and development (R&D), design, marketing and education programme to ensure that the new range was a success.

The decision to convert to organic cotton was based on a strong commitment to the environment rather than on commercial objectives. According to Alison May, Patagonia's President and General Manager,

> when we decided to switch to organic cotton we knew it would be a difficult and risky undertaking . . . Our market research showed that we could possibly lose about 10% of our total sales by dropping conventionally grown cotton from our product line for Spring '96 (May 1995: 3).

She also noted that when the issue was discussed by the Board of Directors their comment was: 'This is not a financial issue. Knowing what we know about the devastation caused by conventionally grown cotton, we need to sever the ties completely and immediately' (May 1995: 3).

Patagonia experienced problems when they tried to find a ready supply of good-quality, organically grown cotton fabric. The R&D team spent a considerable amount of time locating organic growers and forming supply links with manufacturers willing to spin and knit the fibre. This required new skills, because in the past R&D staff had not needed to become involved in the process of creating fabric for their garments.

Market research undertaken concurrently with the development process found that customers purchase Patagonia products because of their quality—durability, functionality, performance and fit. Environmental concerns were less important to customers than quality. As a result of this work, a marketing strategy was structured with two themes:

- The definition of quality was expanded to include the environment.

- The issues associated with pesticides were put in the context of positive messages about available alternatives.

Pricing was difficult because production costs increased across the range by between 15% and 40%. A decision was made to reduce profit margins on most products to keep retail price increases to a maximum of 20%. The new range was launched on target in spring 1996, and sales have been very positive (Chouinard and Brown 1997: 117-29).

*Box 7.1 **Case study: Patagonia organic cotton clothing***

Department of Agriculture. No synthetic chemicals are used: nitrogen is cycled from the air into soil through alfalfa, and weeds are controlled mechanically.

A Swedish company, Verner Frang AB, has been producing organic cotton since the late 1980s. The company contracts more than 80 farmers in Peru to grow cotton organically. The cotton is sold under the brand name 'White Cotton'.

7.1.1.2 Wool

Like cotton, wool has always been regarded (wrongly) as a natural, environmentally sound product. Sheep farming has contributed to land degradation in countries such as Australia, and the processing of raw wool is far from benign. Around two-thirds of the weight of raw wool is grease, dried sweat, skin flakes, dirt and plant matter. The cleaning or scouring process consumes large amounts of water, detergent and chemical solvents and produces heavily polluted waste-water with trace elements of pesticides used on sheep to control lice and flies. In recent years, wool-scouring activities have shifted from developed to developing countries, where environmental controls are less stringent.

Although the environmental impacts of scouring have been reduced in recent years with stricter pollution controls and improved technologies for waste-water treatment, a modern plant with two scouring lines can produce the pollution equivalent of a small city of 60,000 people (Wright 1993: 9). In Australia the Division of Wool Technology of the Commonwealth Scientific and Industrial Research Organisation (CSIRO) has developed a number of innovative processes to control waste, including a technique for removing pesticide residues from grease and lanolin and the development of a 'biological reactor' to reduce the amount of suspended solids in the waste-water from wool scouring.

An example of the life-cycle stages for a woollen garment is shown in Figure 7.1.

7.1.1.3 Hemp

The search for more environmentally friendly textiles has led some designers and consumers back to hemp, a fibre that has been used to make paper, fabric and other products for thousands of years. Agricultural hemp produces negligible amounts of tetrahydrocannabinol (THC), the plant's narcotic compound. Today, hemp is used to manufacture jeans, shirts, underwear, hats and shoes. Adidas launched a sports shoe made from hemp in 1995, calling it simply 'Adidas Hemp'. The aim was to use the popularity of marijuana and hemp to capture the youth market (Hakim 1995). Following complaints from the US government that Adidas was using the name to capitalise on the drug culture, the show was renamed 'Gazelle Natural'.[2]

2   See www.sneakers.pair.com/smokable.htm.

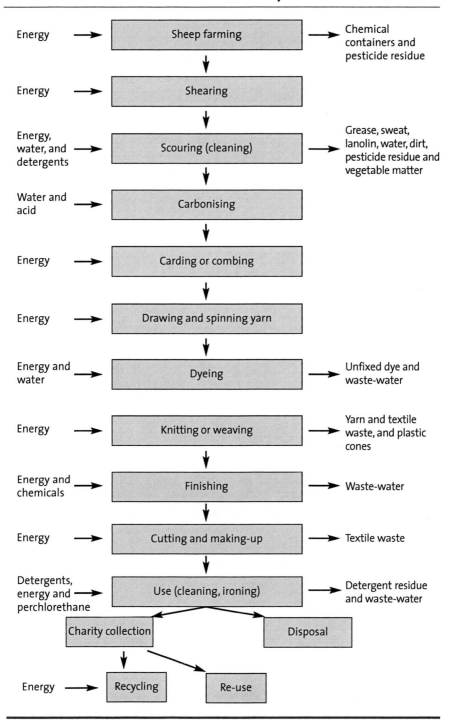

Figure 7.1 **Process tree for a woollen garment**

7.1.1.4 Other natural fibres

Other natural fibres include linen, ramie, kapok, sisal, jute, coir and alpaca fibre. Linen is manufactured from the flax plant. One of the problems associated with flax production is retting, which is the separation of fibres from the plant stalk. This process requires enzymes and water, with environmental impacts such as increased biochemical oxygen demand (BOD) and eutrophication of waterways. Similar problems are experienced with the retting of jute. Fibres such as sisal and coir (from coconuts) are used for woven floor coverings.

The alpaca fibre industry is growing worldwide. According to one industry leader in Australia, alpaca are better suited to the Australian environment than are sheep. They have padded feet so they do not damage the soil, they do not need chemicals for fly strike or foot rot, and each animal can produce up to 12 times more fibre than a sheep (Collis 1999: 18).

7.1.2 Regenerated cellulose fibres

Half-synthetic or regenerated cellulose fibres include viscose, cupro, acetate and triacetate. The cellulose is extracted from wood, and this process has traditionally produced considerable amounts of sulphur compound emissions and polluted water, which requires advanced purification techniques. Some companies are now able to produce so-called solvent-spun fibres in a closed system without sulphur compounds.

The production of a new cellulose fibre by Courtaulds, called Tencel®, uses a solvent (amine oxide) that the company recycles and claims is non-toxic (Paakkunainen 1995: 18).

7.1.3 Synthetic fibres

There is limited information available on the impacts of making petrochemical fibres, which are manufactured from either oil or gas. The production of these fibres uses only a small fraction of the total oil and gas consumed for energy but is linked to all the impacts of the petrochemical industry such as airborne emissions of volatile organic compounds (VOCs). Polypropylene and polyethylene are both energy-efficient and relatively clean to produce and are recyclable in their pure form (when they are without contamination). Polyester can be produced in a closed system and is relatively non-polluting. The manufacture of nylon, a polyamide, may be responsible for significant emissions of nitrous oxide, a greenhouse gas and ozone-depleting chemical (Paakkunainen 1995).

Polyvinyl chloride (PVC) is the target of an international Greenpeace campaign against all chlorine-containing products. Concerns about PVC relate to the possible emission of hydrochloric acid and dioxins during incineration and the production of organochlorine wastes during the manufacturing process.

7.2 Dyeing and finishing textiles

Dyeing and finishing processes can have major impacts on the environment through the use of water, energy and chemicals and emission of waterborne pollutants. Table 7.2 shows some of the important textile chemicals and their relative pollution capability.

Fibre	Process	Electricity (kWh kg⁻¹)	Steam (kg kg⁻¹)	Effluent volume (l kg⁻¹)
Cotton	Cold pad	0.125	0	30
Cotton	Warm exhaust	0.22	4	80
Wool	Hot exhaust	0.08	2	25
Polyester	High temperature	0.15	4.25	32.5

Table 7.2 **Comparison of environmental impacts of dyeing processes**

Source: Dickinson 1997: 3

7.2.1 Dyeing

The main wastes from the dyeing process are contaminated water from dyeing, rinsing and washing baths and from dyeing chemicals. Energy is consumed when heating the dye baths and running pumps and other parts of the dyeing machinery. A comparison of electricity, steam and water effluent losses for different fibre types and dyeing processes is given in Table 7.3.

Cold-pad batch dyeing for cotton has much lower impacts on the environment than have traditional methods. The Australian Dyeing Company adopted this technology for open-width knitted fabric in the early 1990s as part of a major restructuring to reduce costs and improve quality. The traditional process had involved many hours of rough treatment, using lots of chemicals, including bleach and hot and cold water. The new process uses 33% less energy and 45% less water, requires fewer chemicals and produces less effluent. It also requires less floor space and produces a higher-quality product. According to the company, the fabric undergoes less turbulence during a cold-pad batch dyeing process and therefore retains a smooth, uniformly coloured appearance with softer drape and handle.[3]

A designer can reduce the environmental impacts of dyeing by avoiding very dark shades and some colours, such as red and scarlet, that require a large amount of rinsing to remove the unfixed component. Most medium to heavy shades require a long dye cycle that consumes large amounts of energy, water, chemicals and salt.

3 See EnviroNET Australia's Cleaner Production Case Study, at www.environment.gov. au/epg/environet/eecp/case_studies/ausdye.html.

General chemical type	Difficulty of treatment	Pollution category
▪ Alkalis ▪ Mineral acids ▪ Natural salts ▪ Oxidising agents	Relatively harmless inorganic pollutants	1
▪ Starch sizes ▪ Vegetable oils, fats and waxes ▪ Biodegradable surfactants ▪ Organic acids ▪ Reducing agents	Readily biodegradable; moderate–high BOD	2
▪ Dyes and fluorescent brighteners ▪ Fibres and polymeric impurities ▪ Polyacryate sizes ▪ Synthetic polymer finishes ▪ Silicones	Dyes and polymers difficult to biodegrade	3
▪ Wool grease ▪ Polyvinyl alcohol (PVA) sizes ▪ Starch ethers and esters ▪ Mineral oil ▪ Surfactants resistant to biodegradation	Difficult to biodegrade; moderate BOD	4
▪ Anionic and non-ionic softeners ▪ Formaldehyde and N-methylol reactants ▪ Chlorinated solvents and carriers ▪ Catonic retarders and softeners ▪ Biocide sequestering agents ▪ Heavy metal salts	Unsuitable for conventional biological treatment; negligible BOD	5

Category 1: least polluting; category 5: most polluting
BOD = biochemical oxygen demand

Table 7.3 **Chemicals used in textile processing**

Source: Cooper 1990; cited in Paakkunainen 1995: 22

Only a few colours are highly toxic, but most are persistent in nature and have harmful effects on animal and human health. The most toxic are those with azo, triphenylmethane and methine structures. Some dyes contain heavy metals, such as chromium, cadmium, copper, cobalt, zinc and nickel, or require the use of heavy metal-containing mordants. Piece dyeing may reduce the amount of dye used, because cutting leftovers are not dyed, and allows a quick response to changing colour trends (Paakkunainen 1995: 24).

7.2.1.1 Wool

Wool processing may involve toxic solvents such as hexane and perchlorethane, used to clean and finish wool, and poisonous metal salts such as dichromate, used in wool dyeing. Approximately 70% of wool dyeing involves the use of heavy metals, especially for the creation of deep black and navy. The CSIRO has developed a low-chrome dye technique that may assist the industry to meet stricter limits on chromium in waste-water. This involves a two-stage bath-dyeing system that reduces chromium concentrations in the rinse water to 0.05–0.2 parts per million (ppm), 10–15 times lower than the best of conventional one-bath systems, without loss of colour fastness (Wright 1993: 11).

A case study of an environmental line of commercial woollen textiles is given in Box 7.2.

If we understand that design leads to the manifestation of human intention, and if what we make with our hands is to be sacred and honour the Earth that gives us life, then the things we make must not only rise from the ground but return to it, soil to soil, water to water, so that everything that is received from the Earth can be freely given back without causing harm to any living system. This is ecology. This is good design (McDonough 1993).

WHEN DESIGNTEX DECIDED TO CREATE AN ENVIRONMENTAL LINE OF COMMERCIAL textiles several years ago, it used a blend of New Zealand wool and organically grown ramie from the Philippines. Much attention was paid to the selection of dyes that would have minimal impact on the environment. Working with a Swiss textile mill and Ciba-Geigy, it narrowed down the initial list of 4,500 pigments in textile dyes to 16 colours that can be manufactured without release of carcinogenic chemicals, toxic chemicals that bioaccumulate in tissues, heavy metals or mutagenic substances. All colours except black can be produced from the 16 pigments. The textile range was developed and designed with the assistance of William McDonough, a well-known architect and designer (DesignTex n.d.).

Box 7.2 **Case study: DesignTex wool/ramie textiles**

7.2.1.2 Cotton

Natural dyes may be a more environmentally benign alternative for cotton, although Patagonia decided not to use natural dyes in its organic cotton range because it did not meet quality standards. Cotton does not easily bond to dye molecules and toxic metals are required to make the dyes colourfast to light, chlorine, laundering and mechanical abrading (Chouinard and Brown 1997: 23).

Natural dyes may also cause environmental problems of their own because of the risks of ecological damage from collecting large quantities of plants, insects and fungi from the wild.

Naturally coloured cottons may be a better alternative than natural dyes, although the range of colours is restricted. Sally Fox, founder and president of Natural Cotton Colours in Arizona, spent years breeding wild cottons in various shades of green and brown with the superior fibre and agronomic properties of commercial white cotton. The first fibre was sold in 1989, and the range is gradually gaining acceptance in the mainstream textile industry. In addition to its environmental advantages, FoxFibre® is cost-competitive. To produce a pound of a medium shade of brown yarn costs about US$3.96. To produce the same colour using a blend of 50% FoxFibre® with 50% white cotton costs only US$2.72. By eliminating the dye process, which alone costs around US$2, use of the natural cotton results in a saving of 31%. A khaki fabric made with natural cotton costs around 27% less. The higher initial cost of the fibre is more than offset by saving the cost of the dye.[4]

7.2.1.3 Blends and synthetics

Dyeing blended fabrics can have a greater impact on the environment than can the dyeing of single-fibre fabrics. The fabric may need to be dyed twice because the fibres need different dye types. Toxic or carcinogenic carriers are often needed to dye synthetics at low temperatures: for example, in wool blends (Paakkunainen 1995: 26).

7.2.2 Finishing

Many of the finishing treatments used to give textiles special properties have environmental or health problems associated with them. The materials include:

- Resins used to make fabrics shrink-proof, wrinkle-free or less absorbent

- Fire retardants (phosphonates and ammonium salts are safer options that halogen compounds or antimony oxides)

- Metal compounds and organochlorides in finishes against microbial attack and odour

- Chlorophenylide and pyrethroid-based moth-proofing of wool

- Softeners to improve the feel and handling of the fabric

- Aesthetic finishes such as stone washes that use water, energy and chemicals and that weaken the fabric

Although the impacts associated with finishing treatments can be further reduced, one solution is to choose fibres and fabrics that naturally have the desired quali-

4   Natural Cotton Colours Inc., www.foxfibre.com.

ties. Examples include selecting synthetics for easy care and water repellence, cotton for absorbency and aramids or a polymer that has a flame retardant (phosphorus compound) in it for fire resistance. Synthetic acetates are quite resistant to insects and microorganisms (Paakkunainen 1995: 28). When comparing regenerated cellulose fabrics, lyocell is more resistant to shrinkage and wrinkling than is rayon.

7.3 Clothing design and manufacture

One of the most fundamental environmental issues associated with the clothing industry is its focus (and dependence) on ever-changing fashion. Most clothes do not wear out; they simply get replaced by the latest designs and colours. Millions of dollars are spent on marketing the new look each season. This 'design obsolescence' creates a dilemma for any designer trying to address the environmental impacts of their clothing products.

Other environmental issues are those relating to the specification of fabrics, colours and components. The choice of fabric may be between organic and non-organic cotton, or between wool and polyester. The choice of colours has an impact on the type of dyeing and finishing required and therefore on the amount and toxicity of waste in manufacturing.

The choice of components such as zips and buttons can also have an impact. Most buttons are manufactured from plastics, but alternatives with social and environmental benefits are starting to emerge. For example, an organisation called Conservation International sells buttons and jewellery made from the ivory-like tagua nut from Ecuador. The initiative generates jobs and income for local communities and gives them an incentive to maintain their forests.

An example of a range of clothing made with environmental and social issues in mind is given in Box 7.3.

7.4 Maintaining the product during use

The most significant impact of clothing on the environment is during its use, through maintenance activities such as washing, dry-cleaning and ironing. A study by Walsh and Brown (1995) compared the environmental costs, in dollars, of two T-shirts, one made from conventionally grown cotton and one made from organic cotton. Costs were evaluated for each stage of the product life-cycle. The study found that for both T-shirts the stage with the greatest environmental impact was consumer care, accounting for between 70% and 80% of costs.

A number of fabrics such as acetate are not washable and must be dry-cleaned, although some new acetate circular knits are hand-washable. Dry-cleaning involves the use of perchlorethane, a toxic chemical. The US Environmental Protection

IN THE EARLY 1990S ESPRIT ESTABLISHED ITS ECOLLECTION DIVISION, WHICH helped to establish new environmental standards for the clothing industry. The philosophy of the Ecollection was that how something is made is as important as the product itself. Materials and processes were carefully selected for the least environmental impact and the most positive social impact.

Fabrics

All Ecollection cotton items were made from either certified organic or certified transitional organic cotton. Organic linen was also used in sweater yarn and woven vests. Other fabrics used in the collection included Tencel®, manufactured from sustainably harvested wood pulp, and post-consumer recycled Donegal tweed.

Dyes

Natural dyes such as indigo and cochineal were used for linen and cotton sweaters. Indigo comes from the indigo plant, grown in India. The cochineal was produced by beetles on Peruvian cactus farms. Other dyes used were high-fixation synthetic dyes, which reduced the amount of dyestuffs discharged into waste-water.

Finishes

Biodegradable enzyme washes were used to soften and smooth fabrics and prevent pilling. The enzymes were produced by a natural fermentation process. Formaldehyde resins are often used in finishing processes to minimise shrinkage, but formaldehyde is a suspected carcinogen. The Ecollection fabrics were finished with chemical-free alternative processes, which still met industry standards for shrinkage.

The Esprit Ecollection

Components

Metal components such as buckles and zippers are commonly electroplated to produce a rust-proof and decorative finish. The process does, however, generate hazardous sludge. To avoid electroplating, all metal trims on Ecollection garments were made from non-rusting alloys. Buttons were made from a diverse range of environmentally friendly materials, including recycled silver from old photographic film, reconstituted glass from Ghana and Tagua nuts from Ecuador.

Recycling

Fabric scraps generated in the manufacturing process were used to make handmade paper in India. The paper was purchased back to make covers for promotional brochures, which were printed with soy-based ink.

Box 7.3 **Case study: Esprit's Ecollection**

Source: Esprit, Ecollection product brochures, undated

Agency (EPA) is implementing a Garment Textile Care programme, which aims to promote cleaner technologies in the dry-cleaning industry.[5]

The designer should specify washable fabrics to avoid the impacts of dry-cleaning. Often, clothing needs to be dry-cleaned because the lining is not pre-shrunk or because shoulder pads or interlinings are not washable. These problems can be avoided through careful selection of fabrics and making some components such as shoulder pads detachable.

Washing clothing, bed linen and interior textiles also has impacts on the environment through the extensive use of water, energy and detergents. Instructions to the consumer on product care should include reference to less damaging options such as airing, brushing, hanging woollen items outside in moist weather and removing stains as soon as they appear.

Man-made fabrics can often be washed at low temperatures and can be drip-dried, requiring little if any ironing. This can result in enormous energy savings over the life of a product. Consumer education is essential to encourage a sustained shift in behaviour (e.g. by washing in cold water).

Another issue related to the use of a textile product is that of design for durability to extend the life of the product and to minimise the need for repairs. The product should also be designed for reparability wherever possible.

7.5 Waste and recycling

Computerised pattern layout and cutting has reduced the amount of fabric scrap generated during the making of garments and other textile products, although a considerable amount of waste is still generated. This waste should be collected and recycled, where facilities exist.

Fabric scraps are often collected for re-use as rags for automotive and mechanical workshops. They can also be reprocessed into new textiles and other products. For example, denim maker Greenwood Mills in South Carolina processes denim scraps into non-woven home insulation.

Interface Fabrics Group in Maine sell approximately one million lb of textile waste, fibre, yarn, floor sweepings, fabric remnants and so on to a company that produces relief blankets. The company also processes yarn waste and woven fabric into a fibre that can be mixed back into future blends of the same product.

Large quantities of used clothing are collected by charity organisations to provide clothing to the needy and to raise money for welfare work. One charity organisation in Australia, the Smith Family, recycles worn-out clothing that is not suitable for re-use. Their non-woven textile plant has been operating for many years in Sydney, manufacturing cleaning cloths and other non-woven products.

Another recycled textile on the market is EcoFleece®, manufactured from polyethylene terephthalate (PET) soft-drink bottles. The bottles are collected from

5   Go to www.epa.gov/opptintr/dfe/garment/garment.html.

Plate 7.2 **The Marmot Jumper, manufactured by Kathmandu from EcoFleece®**

households and recycling depots, granulated, extruded into polyester filament and spun into a fibre. After undergoing a variety of finishing processes, the fibre is made into knitted, woven and non-woven fabrics (Plate 7.2). Products available from recycled PET include jumpers, bike shorts, socks, rucksacks, thermal underwear, futon filling, webbing and textured woven fabric suitable for luggage and upholstery fabrics. Every jumper manufactured from recycled PET keeps around 25 soft-drink bottles out of landfill, and for every 3,700 2 l bottles recycled, one barrel of oil and half a tonne of toxic air emissions are saved (McLaren 1995: 36). An example of the use of recycled PET to produce panel and upholstery fabrics is provided in Box 7.4.

Covington Industries in the USA introduced its EarthSPUN recycled cotton yarns in 1998. The yarns are manufactured from recycled denim jeans and textile mill waste.

TOLTEC FABRICS IS PRODUCING PANEL AND UPHOLSTERY FABRICS FROM recycled polyester. The polyester fibre is spun from recycled PET soft-drink bottles. According to the company, the challenge in developing fabrics from recycled materials is maintaining consistency and eliminating potential impurities (Sloan 1998: 14).

Toltec is a subsidiary of Interface Inc, an international leader in the shift to more sustainable business practices. The goal is to shift to renewable resources, including to the creation of a 'closed-loop' manufacturing cycle to eliminate waste. Another subsidiary, Interface Flooring Systems, is recycling carpet-backing scrap into a powder that becomes a raw material for the manufacturing process. A 100% recycled carpet product is undergoing evaluation (Interface 1996).

Box 7.4 **Case study: Interface Inc.**

Second-hand clothing is also undergoing a boom in popularity, with 'grunge' fashion trends and the growing acceptability of household recycling contributing to the success of charity and 'retro' clothing stores. A recent headline in a Melbourne newspaper was a sign of the times, claiming that 'Smarter Sleeker Op Shops Buy into the Recycling Revolution' (Webb 1997: 7).

7.6 Issues for designers

Interior and fashion designers need to be aware that textiles have significant impacts on the environment throughout their life-cycle. There are many positive developments in the industry, such as the increasing availability of organically grown cotton and the implementation of cleaner production programmes in manufacturing and dyeing companies. The industry still has a long way to go in becoming truly sustainable, however. A checklist for apparel design is provided in Box 7.5.

Designers can influence manufacturers in a number of ways. First, they can ask their suppliers for detailed information on the chemicals used in fibre and textile manufacture. They can make informed choices and specify use of textiles that can demonstrate environmental benefits. At the same time, they can educate their clients or employers, as well as the consumers, about the environmental choices made.

Some 'eco-friendly' products, such as unbleached cotton, have fairly limited (albeit positive) benefits for the environment. We need to adopt an holistic, life-cycle approach to ecodesign. This needs to involve careful selection of textiles, colours, finishes and components, and design for low-impact maintenance.

It may also involve more complex, non-linear relationships along the supply chain. Lynda Grose notes that some of the successful breakthroughs in the development of organic cotton products in the early 1990s resulted from a more co-operative approach between designers and their suppliers. Designers worked closely with farmers on how to reduce costs, and companies such as Esprit (Box 7.3 on page 142) made pre-harvest commitments to purchase a certain amount of organic cotton. Spinners shared information on which types of cotton were best for which types of fabric.

There are still many barriers to be overcome by environmental designers, such as higher prices for organic cotton. Grose stresses the positive and creative role that can be played by designers in finding solutions to ecodesign problems:

> By acknowledging the potential conflict between environmental objectives, business objectives and creative objectives, and by building bridges from each side without compromising basic principles, innovative solutions can be continuously discovered. We simply need to apply ourselves to the task of creative problem-solving. This is the true essence of design (Grose 1995: 11).

Design

- Aim to make durable clothing
- Strive to design clothing with classic lines that will not go out of fashion
- Design functional garments—for example:
  - Pockets should actually be used and should not be for effect
  - There should be no ornamental components
  - Garments should be sized for comfort not vanity

Choice of fabric

- Consider the use of recycled fabrics with high post-consumer recycled content, such as fabric manufactured from PET bottles or recycled wool
- Consider the use of natural renewable fibres such as cotton, wool and silk
- Consider the use of unbleached fabrics
- Consider the use of chemical-free natural fabrics
- Consider the use of undyed fabrics
- Consider the use of naturally coloured fabrics, such as naturally coloured green or brown cotton
- Consider wherever it is possible to use organic materials
- Investigate alternative fibre sources such as hemp and Tencel®
- Use colourfast synthetic dyes or biodegradable natural dyes, because dyes can leach out during dyeing and washing
- Consider using only natural fabric and components to allow the garment to be composted at the end of its life
- Consider using the same synthetic material for fabric and components so that the garment can be recycled at the end of its life

Choice of components

- Consider the use of natural renewable components, such as buttons and jewellery from tagua nuts from the Amazon rainforest
- Consider the use of recycled and/or recyclable components, such as recycled PET cords, labels and webbings
- Ask material suppliers to provide a comprehensive background on the fabrics and trim so that they will become aware of the product's shortcomings

Production

- Maximise fabric yields and minimise fabric wastage by carefully checking lay plans and garment design
- Consider laying up with re-usable cardboard patterns instead of single-use computer-generated lay-plan paper

Box 7.5 **Apparel design checklist** *(continued opposite)*

Source: adapted from SRD 1997

- Investigate methods of reducing and recycling fabric wastes in the production process

Garment use

- Provide information on fabric content and on care and laundering on permanent garment labelling to educate customers about proper care of their garment
- Avoid use of fabrics or construction detailing that require special laundering such as dry-cleaning
- Educate both retail and end-use customers on the environmental benefits of the garments

Box 7.5 (continued)

◢ Useful websites and agencies

Garment and Textile Care programme

www.epa.gov/opptintr/dfe/garment/garment.html

This page provides details on the US Environment Protection Agency's programme to reduce the environmental impacts associated with the dry-cleaning industry.

HEMPTECH: The Industrial Hemp Information Network   **www.hemptech.com**

This site provides information on products, news, details of books and more.

Natural Cotton Colours Inc.   **www.foxfibre.com**

In addition to marketing naturally dyed cotton products, this site also contains information on the environmental impacts of traditional dyeing techniques.

Textiles Environmental Network (TEN), c/o National Centre for Business and Ecology, Peel Building, University of Salford, Manchester M5 4WT, UK

TEN co-ordinates seminars and publishes a newsletter, Attention.

The Organic Cotton Site   **www.sustainablecotton.org**

This is an excellent site for information on organic cotton production, the impacts of pesticide use, The Organic Cotton Project, case studies and further resources.

Welcome to Patagonia   **www.patagonia.com**

This site contains information about this innovative outdoor equipment and clothing company and about their environmental initiatives (at www.patagonia. com/enviro).

8
FURNITURE

Furniture is coming under increasing environmental scrutiny. A stronger sense of responsibility is building, particularly in the commercial office furniture industry, as designers, furniture specifiers and facilities managers are becoming more aware of the environmental impacts of their products. These impacts are exacerbated by the relatively high rate of 'churn' (i.e. product turnover and movement) that take place as a result of fitting out a new office or reconfiguring an existing one.

Design issues relating to furniture can be divided into two areas. The first critical area is product-specific and relates to ecodesign objectives that need to be addressed wherever practicable, possible and desirable in the design of the product itself (e.g. minimise and consolidate material types, specify commonly recyclable materials and so on).

The second critical area is system-wide and concerns the development and implementation of corporate strategies and services that can exploit many of the product-specific ecodesign features that are likely to be embodied in the product. Such strategies include the development and implementation of a company environmental policy and a product stewardship approach that may incorporate product take-back and leasing services.

Both areas reflect an explicit life-cycle or cradle-to-grave approach and aim to minimise environmental impacts across the product life-cycle—from materials selection and production through to distribution, use, re-use, recycling and ultimate disposal. It is vital that this life-cycle approach permeates the design process to help ensure, for example, that environmental problems seemingly addressed in one component or life-cycle stage do not negatively affect the environmental performance of another component or stage. In reality, ecodesign involves a continuing process of review and trade-offs, with a focus on always aiming to eliminate or minimise the most serious environment problems.

8.1 Selecting materials

Specifying use of environmentally improved materials will rely on pursuing general principles and then evaluating the advantages and disadvantages of specific material types. It should be noted that the relationship between materials and recycling is fluid and that any life-cycle environmental improvement may depend on getting the right mix of solutions. In other words, consideration of materials selection in isolation from the disassembly and recycling process could result in unsuspected environmental problems. More localised life-cycle assessment work during the design process may be necessary to ensure environmental compatibility between materials selection and end-of-life options.

Material quantities should be minimised without compromising function, quality, aesthetics or applicable standards. Environmentally improved materials should be used wherever possible. These could include use of materials:

- With recycled content (preferably post-consumer)

- Made without any toxic or hazardous substances

- Derived from renewable sources

- Commonly recycled and supported by collections systems and product take-back schemes

- That are produced through processes that are not highly energy-intensive

- That do not contribute to 'sick building syndrome' or other indoor air-quality problems (see Section 8.3)

- That are not ozone-depleting

In addition, it could involve:

- Reducing the diversity of material types in order to facilitate more viable end-of-life recycling

- Specifying use of recycled materials in non-critical components where performance, colour, surface design or other visual qualities are not pivotal design features

Wood-based materials should be sourced from sustainably managed plantations and be certified accordingly. Those materials containing toxic or hazardous substances should be avoided, with particular attention to reduced levels of urea formaldehyde.

8.1.1 Recycled materials

Where possible, the designer should specify use of recycled and/or recyclable materials. Recycled materials are used by some furniture designers for environmental and aesthetic reasons. MetaMorf, in Portland, OR, manufactures striking

Plate 8.1 **Outdoor furniture manufactured by MetaMorf from recycled plastics**

chairs, ottomans and cafe tables from recycled plastic (Plate 8.1). Some of the furniture is made from plastic sheets produced in a particle board press that has been modified to handle plastic. The raw material is granulated post-consumer polyethylene.

Wharrington International in Melbourne, Australia, has also developed an innovative process to manufacture furniture from post-consumer acrylonitrile butadiene styrene (ABS) plastic (see Box 8.1).

8.2 Manufacture

Environmental impacts during the production stage can be minimised through the careful specification of materials and processes. This will involve the design team working closely with production staff and suppliers. There are several ways to maximise efficiency and minimise impacts during the production stage, including:

- Reducing the number of components and assemblies
- Eliminating and minimising offcuts, by-products and other materials wastage
- Minimising materials diversity or types
- Integrating functions and simplifying assemblies
- Selecting low-impact materials and cleaner production methods that eliminate or significantly reduce any toxic or hazardous inputs
- Eliminating the use of solvent-based adhesives, coatings and finishes
- Eliminating the use of coatings and finishes that contain heavy metals

A case study is provided in Box 8.2.

WHARRINGTON INTERNATIONAL DEVELOPED A RECYCLED PLASTIC MATERIAL called RECOPOL™ to replace plywood shells for the furniture industry. The raw material is recycled acrylonitrile butadiene styrene (ABS), an engineering-grade plastic resin from used home appliances such as vacuum cleaners, telephones and televisions and from office equipment such as computers and toner cartridges.

The RECOPOL™ shells can be worked in the same fashion as timber (e.g. shaped, sawn, routed, drilled, stapled and nailed) in a manner similar to working high-density timber. Metal fittings can all be moulded into the form. The mouldings can be used to replace wood, plywood, particle board, cast iron, clay, fibreglass and plaster.

Wharrington International has been exploring the formation of closed-loop alliances: for example, by incorporating of granulated toner cartridge waste from the Royal Melbourne Institute of Technology (RMIT) into upholstered tub chairs. This represents a 'close-the-loop' alliance between Wharrington International, cartridge recycler Toner and Ink, and RMIT.

The Re-Define sofa made with RECOPOL™ recycled plastic resin and recycled PET fabric

Box 8.1 **Case study: Wharrington International**

8.3 Use

The use stage of seating is generally a low-impact phase; however, the following objectives should be considered:

- Attention should be given to materials and sensorial qualities that could positively contribute to creating a healthy, vibrant and productive work-space through innovative use of colour, texture, surface design, etc.

- Adjustability and minor repairs should be straightforward so as not to be a contributing factor in premature obsolescence and unnecessary disposal.

One of the most important drivers for change in the commercial furniture industry has been recognition of the environmental and human health hazards

SCHIAVELLO COMMERCIAL INTERIORS DEVELOPED THE PROTOTYPE HOTDESK™
to explore the implications that changing work practices, emerging information technologies and environmental issues may have for the design of commercial office furniture.
The company was one of six participants in the EcoReDesign™ programme at the Centre
for Design, Royal Melbourne Institute of Technology (RMIT).

The Centre for Design conducted research on the nature and extent of changing work
practices and the impact of these changes on furniture design. More flexible work practices
demand a high level of flexibility in furniture design to accommodate changing teams and
mobile personnel.

A life-cycle assessment (LCA) was also undertaken on existing furniture. The study highlighted two general areas of environmental impact in need of reduction or elimination:

- Manufacturing impacts (e.g. use of materials and production processes contributing to toxic or hazardous wastes that might lead to site contamination and
  emissions to air and water)

- Disposal or end-of-life impacts (e.g. contributions to waste to landfill by discarded furniture components and materials that might otherwise be re-used,
  refurbished or recycled)

More specifically, certain hazardous substances used in the pre-treatment of metal
components prior to the powder coating process were identified as an area in need of
ecodesign and cleaner production.

Environmental achievements

The HOTdesk™ prototype (see Plate 8.2) indicates the potential for several areas of environmental improvement. Its new environmental features are likely to result in a product that
is:

- Manufactured with use of cleaner production techniques, particularly in relation
  to the powder coating process for metal components

- More durable and capable of being refurbished, therefore minimising its contribution to municipal solid waste

- Designed for disassembly to enable more cost-effective re-use of components
  and recycling of materials, again minimising its contribution to municipal solid
  waste

- More resource-efficient by using fewer materials overall, therefore minimising
  the potential for waste generation from the outset

- Highly flexible, mobile and reconfigurable, therefore minimising the risk of premature obsolescence that so often results in office furniture going to landfill

- Sensitive to minimising its contribution to indoor air pollution through the elimination or reduction of use of adhesives, solvents and other substances releasing
  volatile organic compounds

Box 8.2 **Case study: Schiavello Commercial Interiors HOTdesk™**

Source: Gertsakis et al. 1997

Plate 8.2 **Schiavello Commercial Interiors HOTdesk™**

associated with emissions of chemicals, such as formaldehyde, nitrogen dioxide, chlorofluorocarbons (CFCs) and volatile organic compounds (VOCs). This is a form of indoor air pollution, which is often referred to as 'off-gassing'.

With people spending up to 90% of their time indoors, indoor air quality has gained great media exposure, and new illnesses such as 'sick building syndrome' are being blamed for significant losses in employee health and productivity.

Many companies overseas are working to reduce components in furniture that emit toxins, odours and suspected carcinogens. Serious health hazards are associated with the application of solvents, dyes, paints and finishes that contain chemicals such as formaldehyde and VOCs.

8.4 Waste avoidance and resource recovery

Products manufactured by Herman Miller, Steelcase and Wilkhahn include office partitions (or screens), storage units, ergonomic chairs and workstations. Such products are directly related to several areas of environmental impact, with problems arising chiefly during manufacture and disposal. It is the disposal or end-of-life stage where solid waste becomes an issue, particularly when significant volumes of furniture are sent to landfill, either because floor plans change or end-users (and their designers) feel they need the latest colours, fabrics or models.

More specifically, the unnecessary disposal of office furniture can contribute towards a reduction in available landfill capacity and associated impacts such as visual degradation. Depending on the coatings and finishes used to colour the metal components, there is also the potential for site contamination at and around landfills (e.g through leaching of heavy metals into aquatic ecosystems) owing to the toxic or hazardous substances used in furniture manufacture. There are also energy costs and emissions associated with the entire process of removing and transporting discarded furniture to landfills. In one way or another, these factors contribute to inefficient use of materials and resource depletion through the discarding of components and materials that could either be re-used in new furniture products or be reprocessed and specified in other types of durable goods.

The ability to extend product life through design for durability, re-use, refurbishment and materials recycling should directly contribute to keeping a product out of the solid waste-stream for more prolonged periods. A hierarchy of eco-design objectives seeks to collectively address issues of waste avoidance and resource recovery, both in terms of overall product (and sub-assemblies) and in terms of discreet materials. The objectives related to this hierarchy fall into the categories of

- Design for durability
- Design for disassembly
- Design for re-use and refurbishment
- Design for materials recycling
- Design for safe disposal

The relationship between material selection and design for waste minimisation can be extremely fluid—sometimes interrelated, sometimes conflicting. Trade-offs may be necessary if re-use becomes a priority over recycling, or the reverse. This fluidity also results in the duplication of some objectives under different categories; for example, design for disassembly objectives relate both to making re-use and refurbishment viable and to improving the efficiencies of materials recycling.

8.4.1 *Design for durability*

The durability of a product can be extended by:

- Identifying and eliminating potential weak points in the design, particularly for operational parts

- Ensuring that the product is designed for likely misuse as well as the intended use

- Design for economically viable service and repair

The designer should specify use of durable materials and avoid colours or designs that may go out of fashion quickly. Design for upgradability has long been a key issue in the design of information technology (IT) equipment, with evidence that white-goods manufacturers (e.g. Miele) are also developing long-life appliances that can be upgraded to take advantage of the latest energy-, water- and detergent-efficient technologies. Upgradability can lead to a commercial advantage, as the customer is locked into buying upgrades from the company rather than a new chair from a competitor. This would be especially relevant to upgrading textiles components.

8.4.2 Design for disassembly

Relatively complex products such as ergonomic seating will need to be disassembled so that components can be easily removed for repair or refurbishment. Similarly, design for disassembly will enable materials to be more easily separated, identified and sorted for recycling. Design for disassembly should also make the product easier to repair and refurbish, by:

- Minimising the number of separate components

- Avoiding glues, metal clamps and screws in favour of 'push, hook and click' assembly methods (e.g. snap fits)

- Making fasteners from a material compatible with the parts connected

- Designing interconnection points and joints so that they are easily accessible for the opening, loosening or separating of components by hand

- Designing the product as a series of easily accessible 'blocks' or modules

- Using in-mould identification symbols for plastic resins (based on ISO 11469 [ISO 2000]).

- Minimising the number of different materials used

- Locating non-recyclable parts in one area that can be quickly removed and discarded

- Locating parts with the highest value in easily accessible places

- Ensuring that assembly and disassembly can take place with simple tools

- Standardising as many elements as possible, thus avoiding tool changes during assembly and disassembly

- Keeping assembly and disassembly methods to a minimum so as to improve efficiency

- Ensuring that fixings and fasteners are easily accessible

- Keeping the number of fixings and fasteners to a minimum

- Designing for ease of separation so that damage to components is eliminated

8.4.3 Design for re-use and refurbishment

Re-usable products tend to have a lower impact on the environment than single-use products. Life-cycle environmental impacts need to be considered in the design process to minimise the impacts that might arise via re-use such as collection, disassembly, assembly, etc. Design for re-use requires:

- That the product is strong enough to withstand repeated service, repair, handling, assembly and disassembly

- The use of in-mould labels rather than paper and plastic labels (which can be washed off or accidentally removed)

It is also important to design re-usable components either for durability or for cost-effective repair.

8.4.4 Design for materials recycling

Design for materials recycling means that materials (as opposed to components) used to manufacture the product could have a secondary use, either for seating or for another product type. When a product is beyond re-use or refurbishment and its original function is no longer viable as a result of changing work practices, obsolescent technology or dated aesthetics there is a critical need to ensure that the following design for disassembly and recycling objectives are embodied in the product:

- The minimum number of material types should be used.

- Larger quantities of a few different material types is to be preferred, making recycling more viable than in the case where four or five different material types are specified in smaller quantities.

- Relevant symbols or codes should be used to identify material types for recycling.

- When disassembled, components should separate into discreet material types without contaminating each other.

- It should be possible to separate and identify material types quickly, safely and without any cross-contamination.

- Metal contamination of plastics on separation should be avoided (i.e. it is better to have plastic contamination of recovered metal and alloy components).

- Use of composites and laminates should be avoided.

- Fixings and fastenings should be used that eliminate cross-material contamination.

- Adhesives dissimilar to the materials being bonded to should be avoided, as a means of further avoiding contamination.

- Any possible potential re-uses of the materials should be established at the design stage where possible.

8.4.5 Design for safe disposal

The product should be designed for safe disposal to ensure that any components or materials that cannot be re-used, refurbished or recycled are treated and discarded safely and in compliance with relevant regulations. Potentially problematic components should be labelled with instructions for safe disposal, decontamination, degassing or general substance identification (i.e. disposal instructions should be provided somewhere on the product or component). Such information should also be provided to end-users and facility managers, including relevant contact details for safe disposal or processing.

It is strongly recommended that no problematic, toxic or hazardous substances, materials or components be specified.

8.5 System-wide issues

The 'greenest' piece of furniture is unlikely to succeed in the market over the longer term unless underpinned by a strong corporate environmental commitment, innovative after-sales service and fact-based marketing and communications materials. Product stewardship should be viewed with the same level of importance as the actual ecodesign objectives if a company wishes to pursue a best-practice approach to environmentally oriented product development. In essence, 'green' products need 'green' systems, and the activities proposed below help fulfill this imperative.

8.5.1 Product stewardship and take-back

In terms of environmental policy and regulation there is now a strengthening position among the majority of developed countries that manufacturers (and their agents) must take a greater role in keeping their products out of the waste-stream when such products reach the end of their lives and are discarded. This means maintaining close and productive relationships with customers beyond the point-of-sale, warranties and service agreements. Product stewardship and extended producer responsibility are the two most commonly used terms that refer to manufacturers positively managing the environmental impacts throughout the life-cycle of their products. The shorthand description for such approaches is usually described as 'product take-back'.

Two noteworthy US furniture companies selling their office furniture products around the world are Herman Miller Inc. and Steelcase Inc. Both companies are based in Michigan and have developed comprehensive environmental programmes aimed at eliminating or minimising life-cycle environmental impacts, particularly those resulting in solid and hazardous wastes. This work includes product stewardship strategies to enable easier reconditioning for a second life and disassembly for materials recovery and recycling.

As early as 1984, Herman Miller was practising producer responsibility primarily through its AsNew programme. This highly developed programme demonstrates how waste minimisation can be successfully blended with serious business objectives:

> Herman Miller formed a subsidiary, Phoenix Design, to buy back and remanufacture its systems furniture products. The AsNew production process combines parts of used furniture with new pieces so systems furniture can be offered at substantial savings. The programme makes use of components that would otherwise be sent to landfills (Herman Miller 1993).

Steelcase has also seen the value of a taking product back and keeping valuable components and materials out of the waste-stream. The company has managed to establish a successful business division based essentially on waste avoidance through re-use. For several years Steelcase has, through its specialist subsidiary, offered its remanufacturing system:

> When our customers are faced with budgetary constraints or environmental concerns, our Revest subsidiary purchases used Steelcase furniture, then refurbishes, refinishes, re-upholsters, and re-sells it. Revest customers save substantially on high quality office furnishings, and have kept thousands of tons of steel, fabric, foam, leather and plastic out of landfills (Steelcase 1993: 4).

Stakeholders are another key part of Steelcase's environmental success, helping to ensure that producer responsibility principles are understood and indeed that there is a realistic sharing of environmental responsibilities by all those involved in the process of designing, making and specifying commercial furniture:

> Being responsible for the environment means taking responsibility for sharing information with our business partners. We do. We work with our dealers and customers, providing the information they need to buy wisely, reduce our impact, and build healthy offices. We share our research findings and our goals with our dealers, architects, design professionals, customers, and students, who want to learn more (Steelcase 1993: 4).

German furniture manufacturers such as Wilkhahn are pushing back the boundaries by developing ergonomic chairs with durability and recyclability in mind (Box 8.3). Design for disassembly principles are embodied in its furniture to help

ALTHOUGH THE COMPLETE RANGE OF WILKHAHN FURNITURE, INCLUDING CHAIRS and tables, aims to address environmental factors, its highest-profile green product is the Picto™ chair (see picture). The Picto™ chair is designed and built to minimise waste in accordance with the waste management hierarchy: reduce, re-use, recycle. The Picto™ is 'built for longevity' as a primary objective, with materials specified that help increase product durability and overall product life. Service and repair also play a key role in helping to keep Wilkhahn chairs out of the waste-stream. Finally, when the chair is beyond repair or no longer required by the first customer, Wilkhahn will take it back and refurbish, re-use components or recycle materials.

The Wilkhahn Picto™ chair

Photo courtesy Wilkhahn Asia Pacific

Box 8.3 **Case study: Wilkhahn's Picto™ chair**

ensure that service and repair, end-of-life remanufacture and materials recycling are not only realised but also add value to the overall enterprise.

In many ways, Wilkhahn is a model of how an environmental philosophy has been successfully integrated into every facet of a company's operations, from product development and manufacturing through to marketing and after-sales service. In 1996 Wilkhahn was recognised for its environmental foresight by being awarded the highly prestigious German Ecology Prize—carrying Europe's largest prize money for attention to ecological issues. Wilkhahn's Picto™ chair was also the first chair to comply with the rigorous requirements of the Dutch eco-label, Milieukeur.

Wilkhahn offers its customers an integrated range of features and services that collectively address waste minimisation without compromising product quality, functionality or performance. The principle of producer responsibility underpinning Wilkhahn's approach stems from its overall company philosophy, as reflected in its three guiding considerations: integrity of the products, fairness in co-operation and responsibility for environmental protection.

The waste minimisation priorities at Wilkhahn are clearly articulated and concentrate on product durability while still enabling straightforward product repair and disassembly, component re-use and materials recycling. Wilkhahn's approach to blending producer responsibility with waste minimisation begins with designing chairs that are durable. Ongoing service and repair support the aim of product longevity:

> In this respect Wilkhahn offer their customers a special service agreement comprising three checks on function and condition, at the place where the furniture is in use—the last check being after five years. Functional defects or damage are recorded in a test report and, if necessary, a proposal for repair and costs is made. In addition, the customer is offered a service hotline by fax or telephone. A general overhaul of office chairs is usually carried out at Wilkhahn's factory in Bad Munder. Older models that are no longer state of the art can, if desired, be brought up to date.
>
> On top of this Wilkhahn guarantee their customers not only that they will take back office chairs no longer useable, but that they will also ensure proper disposal. The chairs are dismantled at our factory, all the parts are sorted into categories of pure-only materials and recycled to meet the desired goal of a material cycle. The best conditions for perfect recycling and re-use of materials in production are naturally to be found at the producers of the original materials themselves. Only very few parts are no longer recoverable and are disposed of at the refuse incinerating plant (Kramer and Ferstera 1995).

In ensuring that environmental actions are integrated both upstream and downstream of the company's own commercial activities, Wilkhahn selects material and component suppliers that are genuinely attuned to progressive waste minimisation strategies and eager to take responsibility for their materials, especially in terms of recycling.

A checklist for furniture design is given in Box 8.4.

Materials

- Minimise material quantities without compromising function, quality, aesthetics or applicable standards
- Use environmentally improved materials wherever possible. This could include use of:
  - Materials with (preferably post-consumer) recycled content
  - Materials void of any toxic or hazardous substances
  - Materials produced with use of cleaner production or pollution prevention techniques
  - Materials derived from renewable sources
  - Materials commonly recycled and supported by collection systems and product take-back schemes
  - Materials that are produced through processes that are not highly energy-intensive
  - Materials that do not contribute to sick building syndrome or other indoor air-quality problems
  - Materials that are not ozone-depleting

  as well as
  - Reducing the diversity of material types to facilitate more viable end-of-life recycling
  - Specifying use of recycled materials in non-critical components where performance, colour, surface design or other visual qualities are not pivotal design features
- Source wood-based materials that are from sustainably managed plantations and that are certified accordingly
- Avoid wood-based materials containing toxic or hazardous substances, with particular attention to using reduced levels of urea formaldehyde
- Specify use of wood-based materials that:
  - Have the highest possible recycled material content
  - Are commonly recycled
- Specify use of metals and alloys that:
  - Are of the minimum quantity required to meet structural and/or functional needs
  - Have the highest possible recycled material content
  - Have a low embodied energy content
- Explore potential for eliminating the use of textiles in some applications or components
- Specify the use of textiles with improved levels of environmental performance; for example, they should be:
  - Post-consumer recycled materials

Box 8.4 **Furniture design checklist** *(continued over)*

- Knitted, woven or dyed with use of cleaner production methods
- Natural fibre sources from sustainable agricultural operations and certified accordingly
■ Consider the implications of refurbishment and recycling when specifying textiles and when designing fastening methods

Manufacture

■ Reduce the number of components and assemblies

■ Eliminate and minimise offcuts, by-products and other materials wastage

■ Minimise materials diversity or types

■ Integrate functions and simplifying assemblies

■ Select low-impact materials and cleaner production methods that eliminate or significantly reduce any toxic or hazardous inputs

■ Eliminate the use of solvent-based adhesives, coatings and finishes

■ Eliminate the use of coatings and finishes that contain heavy metals

Use

■ Give attention to materials and sensorial qualities that could positively contribute to creating a healthy, vibrant and productive workspace through innovative use of colour, texture, surface design and so on

■ Ensure that adjustability and minor repairs are straightforward so that these issues are not a contributing factor in premature obsolescence and unnecessary disposal

Durability

■ Identify and eliminate potential weak points in the design, particularly for operational parts

■ Ensure that the product is designed for likely misuse as well as the intended use

■ Design for economically viable service and repair

Design for disassembly

■ Minimise the number of separate components

■ Avoid glues, metal clamps and screws in favour of 'push, hook and click' assembly methods (e.g. snap fits)

■ Make fasteners from a material compatible with the parts connected

■ Design interconnection points and joints so that components are easily accessible for opening, loosening or separating by hand

■ Design the product as a series of easily accessible 'blocks' or modules

■ Use in-mould identification symbols for plastic resins (based on ISO 11469 [ISO 2000])

■ Minimise the number of different materials used

Box 8.4 (from previous page; continued opposite)

- Locate non-recyclable parts in one area that can be quickly removed and discarded
- Locate parts with the highest value in easily accessible places
- Ensure that assembly and disassembly can take place with simple tools
- Standardise as many elements as possible thus avoiding tool changes during assembly and disassembly
- Keep assembly and disassembly methods to a minimum so as to improve efficiency
- Ensure that fixings and fasteners are easily accessible
- Keep the number of fixings and fasteners to a minimum
- Design for ease of separation so that damage to components is eliminated

Recycling

- Specify the minimum number of material types
- Use relevant symbols or codes to identify material types for recycling
- Ensure separation and identification of material types can be conducted quickly, safely and without any cross-contamination
- Avoid metal contamination of plastics on separation (i.e. it is better to have plastic contamination of recovered metal and alloy components
- Avoid the use of composites and laminates
- Use fixings and fastenings that eliminate cross-material contamination
- Avoid adhesives dissimilar to the materials being bonded to as a means of further avoiding contamination
- Establish any possible potential re-uses of the materials at the design stage where possible

Disposal

- Label potentially problematic components with instructions for safe disposal, decontamination and de-gassing
- Avoid use of problematic, toxic or hazardous substances, materials or components

Box 8.4 (continued)

9 ELECTRONIC AND ELECTRICAL PRODUCTS

9.1 Introduction

Electronic and electrical products (EEPs) encompass a vast range of goods, from computers to refrigerators. Often the most significant environmental impact of these products from a life-cycle perspective is the energy they consume during their use.

Other environmental issues for EEPs include the impact of materials used in manufacture and product waste at the end of the item's useful life. A number of materials in these products are banned, such as chlorofluorocarbons (CFCs) in fridges and polychlorinated biphenyls (PCBs) in transformers. Other materials are under scrutiny, such as halogenated flame retardants, lead and polyvinyl chloride (PVC). Manufacturers of EEPs are also under increasing pressure from regulatory bodies throughout the world to take responsibility for these products when they become waste. Strategies to reduce waste include increasing the product's durability and designing for disassembly and recycling.

Like all products, EEPs have negative environmental impacts, but they may also help society move toward sustainable development. The dematerialisation concept (replacing products with services) often requires the use of high technology. For example, the use of digital photography allows photos to be taken, shared and printed out with the use of less chemicals and waste than traditional methods.

The three strategies discussed in this chapter are:

- Selecting low-impact materials
- Maximising energy and water efficiencies
- Designing for waste minimisation

9.2 Selecting low-impact materials

The environmental impacts of materials used in EEPs need to be considered at the different stages of the product's life-cycle, from manufacturing through to use and final disposal. There are different risks associated with each of these stages: for example, some materials in batteries may be safe during use but can cause problems when disposed of into landfill or an incinerator.

Material restrictions affecting products come from regulations, eco-labels and customer requirements. It is important to understand those regulations or customer requirements that relate to materials that are currently restricted, those that are being phased out and those that may be used only under certain circumstances.

A useful consolidated source of restricted substances in EEPs was developed by the European Association for Standardising Information and Communication Systems (ECMA), which is a European-based industry association. An ECMA working committee was established to define product-related environmental attributes for information and communications technology (ICT) and consumer electronic products. Their report recommends environmental and end-of-life parameters for inclusion in data sheets and specification sheets and provides examples of product declarations. The information is derived from regulations and the strictest eco-labels.

According to ECMA (1997: 6), a declaration should be made for at least the following substances, to state that they are not present in concentrations exceeding natural background levels:

- Asbestos
- Cadmium (in plastic materials, packaging and inks and in cathode ray tubes)
- CFCs and/or hydrochlorofluorocarbons (HCFCs)
- Chloroparaffins with chain length 10–13 carbon atoms, with chlorination greater than 50% contained (in mechanical plastic parts heavier than 25 g)
- Lead (in mechanical plastic parts heavier than 25 g)
- Mercury
- PCBs or polychlorinated triphenyls (PCTs)
- Polybrominated biphenyls, their oxides and their ethers (in mechanical plastic parts heavier than 25 g)

The presence of listed substances that *do* exceed natural background levels should be declared.

A key law that will effect the use of substances in these products is the European Directive on Waste from Electronic and Electric Equipment as approved by the Council of Ministers on 13 June 2001. This will restrict the use of cadmium, lead, halogenated flame retardants and mercury in electronics products. The law is expected to be in place by 2006, with the restrictions in force by 2008.

A case study illustrating how appliance manufacturer Electrolux avoided the presence of cadmium in a new vacuum cleaner is presented in Box 9.1.

IN SWEDEN ELECTROLUX MANUFACTURES A PORTABLE VACUUM CLEANER with rechargeable, cadmium-free batteries. Cordless appliances requiring high power have previously used nickel–cadmium (NiCd) or lead–acid batteries. An Electrolux development team adapted the latest nickel metal hydride (NiMH) batteries for a rechargeable hand-held vacuum cleaner.

The new application for NiMH batteries was the result of a joint effort between Electrolux and a battery manufacturer. Until recently, all efforts to obtain NiMH batteries for applications with a higher power demand have failed. Either the life-cycle of the battery was shortened or the motor power of the product was lowered compared with using traditional NiCd batteries.

At this time, compared with NiCd, the NiMH batteries are more expensive. This additional cost is compensated for by avoiding the Swedish environmental levy for NiCd batteries. The final price of the new hand-held vacuum cleaners will therefore remain the same. NiMH prices might decrease in the future. The batteries may use the Nordic Swan eco-label. The Nordic Swan has also been used for NiMH batteries for mobile telephones.

Hand-held vacuum cleaners with the new NiMH batteries have strong suction power. They stay charged longer than the old NiCd technology. Another positive aspect is that to maintain their capacity the NiMH batteries do not need to be fully discharged (run down) before they can be recharged—unlike NiCd batteries.

NiCd batteries contain a significant amount (15% by weight) of the heavy metal cadmium, a health hazard that has a negative impact on the environment. Among the health hazards are human skeletal decalcification, lung cancer, and kidney and liver damage. Lead, another hazardous heavy metal, can also be avoided by using the NiMH technology. Lead is used in older types of rechargeable lead–acid batteries.

The annual world consumption of cadmium for small, rechargeable NiCd batteries (used mainly for portable consumer appliances) is about 8,500 tons, of a total of 16,000 tons cadmium produced worldwide. For industrialised countries, the ratio of cadmium used for batteries is higher. For several countries, more than 85% of the industrial use of cadmium is for NiCd batteries (e.g. in Japan and Sweden). In those countries, cadmium use has been restricted for all applications except batteries.

Similar models will soon be introduced in other countries under the Electrolux brand name. Electrolux is now adapting the technology to other rechargeable appliances. Since the demand for cordless appliances is increasing rapidly, the new battery technology will make a major contribution to reducing stress on the environment.

Box 9.1 **Case study: Volta Minette Power Plus**

Source: EGEA 1997

9.3 Maximising energy and water efficiencies

Life-cycle assessment (LCA) studies have shown on many occasions that the largest impact that an electrical or electronic product has on the environment is during its use. This is particularly true for products that use energy and other

Plate 9.1 **The Global range of Dishlex dishwashers set new benchmarks for energy and water efficiency with a six-star energy rating.**

resources during their operation, such as hot water systems, heaters, cooking equipment, fridges, lights, air conditioners, and washing and drying machines. These products collectively use 95% of the energy in an average house (ACA 1992: 21). Studies of products that do not consume significant amounts of energy, such as mobile phones, have often shown that their greatest environmental impact is during manufacture. This is because of the energy-intensive operations required to make components such as silicon chips (Nokia 1999).

Figure 9.1 shows that the energy required for the manufacture of key computer components is substantially less than that required during use of the computer throughout its life (MCC 1993: 9).[1] The new Apple® Power Mac G4™ computer has been designed to achieve significant savings in energy use (Box 9.2).

The environmental and economic impact of energy used by products during their use is also highlighted in a study undertaken as part of the US Energy Star®

---

1 The study was based on the following assumptions: the computer workstation was assumed to be operating 24 hours a day, 7 days a week; the product life (before obsolescence) was estimated at 4 years, although the anticipated life is much longer; energy use during the product life was, therefore, assumed to be 35,000 hours; and the four stages of the manufacturing process include semiconductor devices, semiconductor packaging, printed wiring board and the display.

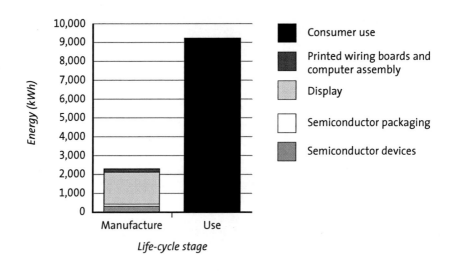

Figure 9.1 **Energy required for key life-cycle stages of a computer**

programme. In 1997, the US Department of Energy (DOE) conducted a study to determine the impact of new clothes washer technology in a real-world setting (Tomlinson and Rizy 1998). In Bern, KS (population 204), the DOE carefully monitored energy and water consumption of 103 clothes washers over two months to gather baseline information about resource consumption. Each of these clothes washers was then replaced by a high-efficiency Energy Star® washer provided by Maytag. Energy and water use data was collected for an additional three months. In all, the study encompassed more than 20,000 loads of laundry and nearly 70 tons of washing.

The results showed dramatic decreases in water and energy use with the new washers. Average water consumption fell from 41.5 gallons per load in the first part of the study to 25.8 gallons per load in the second part of the study—a saving of 38%. Energy consumption, including washer energy and hot water heating, fell by 58%. Further, the moisture content of clothes fell by 7%, meaning less energy was consumed by the clothes dryer—improving overall savings even more. Finally, extensive satisfaction data was collected from the study participants that indicated that the cleaning performance of the new washers was generally superior to the original machines that they replaced (Tomlinson and Rizy 1998).

Dutch electronic giant Philips has developed a new GreenChip™ to reduce power wasted by televisions, video recorders, computers and fax machines working in 'standby' mode. The chip reduces the energy required by products in standby mode from 10 W to 0.1 W. If the US$2.50 chip were to be adopted worldwide it could greatly reduce greenhouse gas emissions.

Standby mode allows devices to be switched on quickly after a long period of inactivity, but this convenience comes at a cost. Philips estimate that US home-

THE POWER MAC G4™ DESKTOP COMPUTER IS APPLE'S DESKTOP COMPUTER released in 1999, based on the PowerPC G4™ microprocessor. The PowerPC G4™ is the first microprocessor that can achieve one billion floating point operations per second (a giga-flop), increasing the speed for completing complex tasks such as in Photoshop filters. The Power Mac G4™ desktop computer can achieve a theoretical peak performance of 3.6 gigaflops.

The Power Mac G4™ uses less than 5 W in 'sleep state'. This is 17% of the 30 W required in the current US Environmental Protection Agency (EPA) Energy Star® criteria. This reflected the design team's aim to build a computer that would consume no more power than a night-light, having little impact on user's energy costs. The expected power consumption of the Power Mac G4™ desktop computer at US voltages (115 V at 60 Hz) is as follows:

The Apple® Power Mac G4™
Photo courtesy of Apple

- On: 45 W
- Sleep mode: 5 W
- Off: 3 W

Figure 9.2 compares energy savings per annum for the Power Mac G4™ desktop computer, a non-Energy Star® computer and an Energy Star®-compliant computer. It shows that the Power Mac G4™ offers considerable energy savings—using 59% less energy than the Energy Star®-compliant computer.

The running costs of these computers per year is shown in Table 9.1 for the US and for a comparative European market (Germany), where energy prices are higher.

Table 9.2 shows the potential energy and monetary savings of the Power Mac G4™ desktop computer over a year compared with standard non-Energy Star®- and Energy Star®-compliant computers for a single unit, for 10,000 units and for 1 million units.

Box 9.2 **Case study: Apple® Power Mac G4™**

Source: Sweatman *et al.* 2000

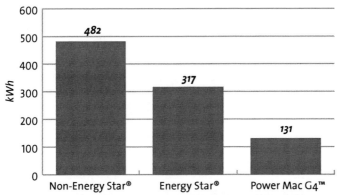

Note: Non-Energy Star® computer assumed to be operating at 55 W without a sleep mode; Energy Star®-compliant computer assumed to be operating at 55 W in active mode and 30 W in sleep. The figures also assume 24-hour, 7-day-a-week operation with 75% of time spent in sleep mode and 25% active.

Figure 9.2 **Energy use per annum of non-Energy Star®-compliant, Energy Star®-compliant and Apple® Mac G4™ computers**

	USA (US$)	Germany (DM)	Germany (US$)
Cost of energy per kWh	0.077	0.31	0.17
Non-Energy Star®	37.11	149.42	81.94
Energy Star®	24.41	98.27	53.89
Power Mac G4™	10.09	40.61	22.27

Table 9.1 **Running costs of non-Energy Star®-compliant, Energy Star®-compliant and Apple® Mac G4™ computers**

	Energy savings (kWh)			Money savings					
				USA (US$)			Germany (DM)		
Number of units used	1	10,000	1×10^6	1	10,000	1×10^6	1	10,000	1×10^6
Non-Energy Star®	351	3.51×10^6	351×10^6	27.02	270,200	27.02×10^6	108.81	1,088,100	108.81×10^6
Energy Star®	186	1.86×10^6	186×10^6	14.32	143,200	14.32×10^6	57.66	576,600	57.66×10^6

Table 9.2 **Potential energy and monetary savings of the Power Mac G4™ desktop computer compared with non-Energy Star®-compliant and Energy Star®-compliant computers**

owners spend US$1 billion each year on powering televisions and video recorders on standby. If all these appliances were to use GreenChips™, 99% of this energy could be saved. In Britain, the new receivers required for digital television could consume the entire output of a 500 MW power station (Fox 1998: 7).

9.3.1 Energy labels

Many eco-labels have requirements for energy efficiency in electrical and electrical products, such as the German Blue Angel and the Nordic Swan eco-labels. There are also specific energy labels in Europe, the USA and Australia, as outlined in Table 9.3. More information on design strategies for energy and water conservation is provided in Section 4.4.

9.4 Design for waste minimisation

The growing number of EEPs in the market translates into substantial amounts of waste entering the waste-stream. This waste includes metals, plastics, glass,

Energy label	Summary of system	Products covered
US EPA Energy Star®	Energy Star® is a collaboration between the US Environment Protection Agency (EPA) and many companies, and is designed to prevent pollution by helping consumers buy products that use less energy. Products such as major appliances qualify for the Energy Star® by meeting minimum standards for energy consumption set by the US Federal government. Products for which there are no minimum energy use standards (such as office equipment) qualify for the Energy Star® if they have special features that enable them to use less energy than similar products.	▪ Heating and cooling appliances ▪ Lighting ▪ Televisions and video recorders ▪ Office equipment ▪ Windows ▪ Exit signs
EU Energy Label	Established in 1995, the European (EU) Union Energy Label is a mandatory system for white goods. The system uses seven grades of energy efficiency, from A, the most economical, to G. The energy label not only indicates the consumption of energy, but also contains information about the use performance of the product. For example, washing machine labels include information on washing performance and water consumption per cycle. Information on noise levels of the product is not mandatory but is often found on the labels.	▪ Fridges ▪ Freezers ▪ Washing machines ▪ Tumble dryers
Australian energy rating system	A joint state government and industry programme, it is compulsory for manufacturers to put an energy rating label on every applicable product. The label shows: ▪ The actual energy consumption under test conditions (a number, usually in kWh per year) ▪ A corresponding star rating: the more stars, the more energy-efficient the appliance	▪ White goods ▪ Heating and cooling appliances ▪ Windows ▪ Houses

Table 9.3 **Energy label systems as used in Europe, USA and Australia**

Plate 9.2 **The Kambrook electric kettle was designed for disassembly and recycling.**

composites and other materials. Not only does this waste place a burden on waste management facilities but also it can sometimes be considered hazardous. Governments and industry are currently developing programmes to take back these products to reduce this environmental problem.

A range of regulations is being proposed for end-of-life product management around the world. In Japan, a rule will come into force in 2001 requiring industry to develop take-back schemes for four product groups (televisions, air conditioners, refrigerators and washing machines). The European Union (EU) is also expected to introduce requirements by 2006 for product take-back through the Directive on Waste from Electrical and Electronic Equipment. In some European countries such rules are already in force (notably the Netherlands, Denmark, Norway, Switzerland and Sweden). The economic and design ramifications of such rules are expected to be significant.

For some products there are opportunities for both reconditioning and re-use, as well as recycling of component materials such as steel and some plastics. Reconditioning extends the life of the product and therefore reduces waste. If the product is no longer repairable, or if the technology lags behind energy-efficient and water-efficient products, it is vital to keep them out of the waste-stream and to recycle as many of the constituent materials as possible.

A hierarchy of strategies relevant for electrical and electronic waste minimisation is:

■ Design for dematerialisation

■ Design for durability

■ Design for upgradability

■ Design for remanufacturing

■ Design for recycling

9.4.1 Design for dematerialisation

Weight reduction is a critical objective in the design of any product. It reduces the cost of manufacture, saves resources and energy and there is less material to be recycled or disposed of at the end of a product's life. System miniaturisation, a long-time trend in the electronics marketplace, is very evident in the computer industry, where the size of products has been halved every five to seven years.

9.4.2 Design for durability

By designing products to last longer it is possible to reduce both resource use and waste generation. The broad concept of durability is to keep a product functional, efficient and culturally relevant for a longer period than most consumers have come to expect. In some cases, however, durability may have an adverse effect on the environment by reducing the adoption of environmentally desirable technological innovations such as increased energy efficiency.

Understanding why products are discarded in the first place is important in developing strategies for product life extension. Two keys reasons for the discarding of products are:

■ Defect or wear-out

■ Product obsolescence

9.4.2.1 Defect or wear-out

Defect or wear-out is the main reason for replacing appliances (Antonides 1990). The occurrence of defects appears to be dependent on the age of the good, the purchase price and the size of the household using the good.

Rising service costs in relation to purchase is one of the main contributors to the replacement of products in preference to repair (Lund 1975). The prices of consumer durable goods fell, on average, by 17% in the USA between 1955 and 1973, whereas the cost of household services rose by 106% (BLS 1974). A similar trend has been evident in Australia, where the cost of a toaster in 1960 was the equivalent of Aus$200, but today most toasters sell for under Aus$50 (ACA 1993: 16-17).

9.4.2.2 Product obsolescence

In addition to product breakdown, technical and stylistic changes can result in products being considered obsolete while they are still perfectly operational. The concept of planned technical obsolescence is a highly debated issue that is difficult to substantiate (Teitenberg 1988: 191). A greater concern regarding obsolescence is the constant changes to products that are often purely stylistic without any foundation in technical innovation (Baillon and Ceron n.d.).

According to Dieter Rams, the head of design at Braun, 'The purchase attraction on which design today is almost exclusively based, and which only fuels the destructive product extravagance, will give way to an aesthetic that supports long term use' (Tuohy 1993: 12).

9.4.2.3 Design for durability

Many products are so designed that when one component fails the entire product is thrown away. This is partly a result of the nature of the product materials and their design: when seals on plastic jug kettles fail, or a moulded-in plug is damaged on any item, the product cannot usually be repaired.

Durability can be enhanced by the use of high-quality materials and by improving reparability (e.g. through modular construction or separable joining techniques). Durability can also be improved through greater availability of spare parts.

Design for durability is also about changing consumer attitudes. Changing fashion trends, seductive advertising and affordable prices may encourage consumers to prematurely replace products that are still useful. The Eternally Yours Foundation in the Netherlands attempts to address this by searching for solutions to reduce consumer desire for new goods and to make consumers want to retain products for longer periods.

9.4.3 Design for upgradability

Upgradable design is suitable for short-life electronic products that are undergoing rapid change or for products that are composed of separable units. The difficulty with modular designs, particularly with longer-life products, is the ability to predict change that can be incorporated into such a design. Modular design systems can provide a common platform on which successive generations can be built. Design that considers modularity can also result in long-term savings to the consumer.

Upgradable design is particularly relevant to products that are undergoing rapid technological change such as computers (see Boxes 9.3 and 9.4). The developments in the computer industry show the potential of modular systems that could be developed in domestic appliances.

Appliance manufacturer Miele has recognised the need to upgrade products to take advantage of new technology with longer-life products. Miele introduced the possibility of modifying programmes on domestic appliances via an optical interface to adapt machines to future developments such as programmes that reduce

JAPANESE COMPUTER MANUFACTURER NEC HAS BASED A RANGE OF NOTEBOOK computers on an upgradable and flexible design. This enables the computer to be upgraded by the addition of new screens, hard drives and memory capacity through interchangeable modules. Inflexible computers that cannot be upgraded can cost far more than a modular model in the long term (Lowe 1993: 25). For example, a notebook that costs $3,500 today could cost more than $17,000 if it cannot be readily upgraded (Firth 1993: 27). The theory is that a cheap notebook will cost more in the longer term because it is likely that the owner will not be able to upgrade and will therefore need to purchase new machines as the technology is superseded.

Box 9.3 **Case study: NEC upgradable notebook**

THE HANDSPRING COMPANY, MAKER OF THE VISOR HAND-HELD COMPUTER, have used upgradability to make it easier, elegant and even fun to expand such devices. Handspring have created the Springboard expansion slot, an open-faced, communication-ready slot designed to easily fit a broad range of accessories, called Springboard expansion modules.

The Springboard upgradability design philosophy states that (Handspring 1999: 3):

- The Springboard expansion slot had to be designed from a user's perspective, not an engineer's perspective.

- A user wishing to add a hardware accessory to a hand-held computer wants an obvious, simple and robust attachment mechanism. No tools or special skills should be required to attach a modem, radio or MP3 player. Once attached, the combined hand-held computer and accessory should be cosmetically and physically integrated.

- Adding or removing an accessory should never require rebooting or resetting the computer. The computer shouldn't need to be in a special state or mode to add or remove an accessory. You should be able to attach and detach an accessory at any time, even while it is in use, without crashing or compromising the system.

- All the software required to use the accessory should be included in the accessory itself. There should be no need to copy software from a disk or PC onto the hand-held computer to use the accessory.

- Springboard expansion modules should be self-installing and de-installing. Attaching and detaching the module should be the extent of user involvement.

Box 9.4 **Case study: Handspring Springboard expansion system**

consumption levels (water, electricity, detergent) and through new laundry-care technology. The first upgrade, which became available in 1998, reduces water consumption by 4 l in some wash programmes.

Many products that traditionally have been modular are now being integrated into single units. Traditionally, a hi-fi has been a collection of separate modules such as a tape player, an amplifier and a tuner, etc. These components are now being integrated into one unit, therefore making it difficult to upgrade or repair any one part (ENDS 1992: 14).

9.4.4 Design for remanufacturing

Remanufacturing is the restoration of used products, or components, to a condition that has performance characteristics similar to those of new products. It results in product life extension and promotes the re-use of components and materials. Remanufacturing is widely used for commercial products such as photocopiers, but is rarely used for domestic electrical and electronic products.

Laser printers and photocopiers have a range of components that are suitable for remanufacturing. Xerox Corporation, for example, remanufactures many of its parts, such as electric motors. Through this programme Xerox is now saving over US$200 million per year by recycling 1 million components for replacement parts and new equipment.

Remanufacturing is relatively uncommon in domestic products, except for a few independent remanufacturers. This is attributed to:

- The decentralised and unpredictable market and supply for used goods

- The rapid change in technology associated with some products

- High transport costs

- Customer prejudice against rebuilt products

Remanufacturing in domestic products tends to be concentrated in the area of power tools, vacuum cleaners and garden and leisure equipment. This is because the effects of styling in these areas are minimal (Henstock 1998: 113).

9.4.4.1 Remanufacturing processes

Companies that remanufacture can be divided into three types:

- Original equipment manufacturers (OEMs). OEMs often make and sell new and remanufactured versions of the product.

- Independent remanufacturers. These companies purchase unserviceable products and remanufacture them for sale.

- Contract remanufacturers. These companies refurbish products under contract to a customer, who retains ownership of the product.

Remanufacture occurs after the sale and trade-in of a product that cannot be serviced. The process that products undergo for remanufacture are (Lund 1984: 18-29):

● Disassembly and cleaning

● Refurbishment of component parts

● Reassembly and testing

Component refurbishment may take a number of forms:

● Surface cleaning and preparation are almost standard.

● Worn areas are often built up by application of weld metal and then machined to original dimensions.

● Holes that wear has made 'out of round' may be bored to oversize in order to accept an insert having the correct internal diameter.

● Bent shafts are straightened.

● Electrical wiring is cleaned and reinsulated.

● Precision surfaces are re-ground and scraped.

A case study of remanufactured cameras is provided in Box 9.5.

9.4.5 Design for recycling

Recycling is the process of recovering materials from products for a second use. Recycling of materials such as metals has been an established process for a considerable period of time; however, as the use of plastics becomes more popular in EEPs, there is a growing interest in how best to recycle these materials.

Recycling is generally done through one of two methods:

● Shredding, to recover the steel

● Disassembly and recycling to recover metals and some other materials

9.4.5.1 Shredding

The process of shredding a product involves a number of steps (Makower 1993: 6):

● Toxic and hazardous substances, such as CFCs and PCBs, are removed and reclaimed or disposed of safely.

● Appliances are put through the shredder (this typically takes only 30 seconds).

● Magnets then capture the steel, which is sent to mills for reprocessing.

● Other metals are sorted, to recover copper, brass and aluminium.

● The remaining materials—mainly plastics, rubber, glass and wood (referred to as residuals or fluff)—are generally sent to landfill.

BY LEVERAGING CUSTOMER RELATIONSHIPS WITH PHOTO-FINISHERS AROUND the world, Kodak has established a variety of marketing and promotional programmes to get single-use cameras back to the company once the customer's film had been removed.

A remanufacturing rate of 70% has been achieved in the USA and approximately 60% worldwide, which compares favourably with the recycling rate for aluminium cans, which was 66.5% in the USA in 1997.

The remanufacturing and recycling process involves a number of stages:

- Cameras are shipped at the rate of millions per month from photo-finishers around the world to one of three collection facilities. Cameras arrive in recyclable cardboard boxes and are first sorted according to manufacturer. Industry-level exchange partnerships have been established by Kodak with Fuji, Konica and other manufacturers. Through these partnerships, Kodak accepts competitors' cameras, and vice versa.

- The Kodak cameras are shipped to a subcontractor facility for processing. There, all packaging is removed along with the front and back covers and any batteries. The cameras are then cleaned in an ionised-air vacuum system and fed to an assembly line of workers. As the cameras move along the lines, they undergo visual inspection. Old viewfinders and lenses are replaced with new ones for quality purposes. For flash models, fresh batteries are inserted. Many small parts are re-used, including the thumb-wheels for advancing the film and the counter-wheels for keeping track of exposures taken. The entire camera frame, metering system and flash circuit board are re-used following rigorous quality testing.

- The sub-assemblies are shipped to one of Kodak's three single-use camera manu-facturing plants. The sub-assemblies are now ready for final assembly into the new product. This process includes loading and pre-winding a fresh roll of Kodak film, adding a new Kodak battery to flash models, installing a new outer package made from recycled materials (with 35% post-consumer content) and finally adding the appropriate outer packaging. The camera is now ready for shipment to the customer.

- Meanwhile, the plastic camera covers pass through a metal detector to be sure no traces of metal are left, and the plastic is shipped to a centre to be re-ground into flake. These plastic pellets are then remoulded into cameras or other products. Discarded packaging for the camera is sent to a paper recycling centre.

Recently, Kodak designed special labels for the Kodak Max single-use camera that are 100% recyclable. The labels are made from a squeezable opticite material that has high-quality printing and adhesion characteristics and that can also be re-ground, pelletised and recycled along with the front and back covers. This makes the labels fully compatible with the recycling stream; therefore photo-finishing laboratories can avoid the time-consuming steps of removing the labels as they extract the film.

Additionally, the batteries that are removed from the recycled cameras are tested and, if good, are used in one of several ways. Many are used internally at Kodak, such as in employee pagers. Others are donated by the company to various organisations as part of a gifts-in-kind programme. Some are sold through third parties on the wholesale or retail markets as recycled batteries. Kodak's policy is not to re-use batteries for new single-use cameras in order to meet customer's expectations of rapid flash recycle time during picture taking.

By weight, 77%–86% of Kodak single-use cameras can be recycled or re-used. Since Kodak began the programme in 1990, it has recycled more than 200 million cameras.

Box 9.5   **Case study: remanufacturing Kodak single-use cameras**

Source: Kodak 1997, www.kodak.com

Plate 9.3 **Miele Appliances: a long history of design for
disassembly and recycling**

Photo courtesy Miele Australia

Shredding is ideal for recovering metals in products; however, as plastics and other materials are more widely used, the residuals will have to be utilised to a greater degree. Alternatively, products will have to be disassembled prior to their metal content being recovered.

Another reason for the greater development of recycling through disassembly is that appliances that do not have a high metal content are not economically viable for the shredding process. Such appliances will therefore require disassembly to recover their materials.

Design for metals recovery is described in detail in *Design for Recyclability*, by Henstock (1988). Strategies include:

- Increasing the use of metals

- Avoiding self-contaminating combinations of materials (e.g. contamination of steel with copper can reduce the value of steel)

- Avoiding toxic substances such as cadmium, asbestos and mercury which may not be accepted for shredding

A possible threat to scrap metal recycling of appliances is the introduction of plastics. Some white-goods manufacturers and the steel industry are now actively encouraging the continued use of metals to ensure that the recycling of these appliances continues (Hunt 1991: 21-24). However, it is unrealistic that appliances will return to being all metal. Plastics have enabled advances in appliance design, such as the creation of products that carry a reduced risk of electrocution (Baillon and Ceron n.d.).

9.4.5.2 Disassembly

Complete product recycling is still in its infancy; however, it is becoming more common as a result of product take-back legislation and companies developing take-back policies. To make disassembly efficient, new recycling processes and designs that are easier to recycle are now being developed.

Recycling through disassembly is the process of recovering components and materials for re-use and recycling. This includes plastics and other complex materials. Owing to the complex nature of many products, this is usually a manual operation.

Industries that have developed recycling through product take-back are centred mostly in Europe because of impending laws (Johnston 1993: 10-13). Companies that have developed appliance recycling outside of Europe have done so as a result of consumer pressure and as a cost-effective alternative to disposing of hazardous waste.

Appliance manufacturers such as Grundig, which is now actively recycling products in Germany, are finding the disassembly process is not cost-effective for complex products such as televisions. Therefore development of efficient recycling processes and re-evaluation of existing designs is a vital step towards reducing this cost (Fox 1993: 20).

An example of an operation that operates successfully is that of British Telecommunications (BT) in the UK (Box 9.6).

9.5 Challenges for the future

The electronics and electrical sector has achieved great progress in some areas—for example, in eliminating some ozone-depleting substances and achieving greater energy and water efficiency. Consumers now are able to select from a range of

IN LINE WITH THE BRITISH TELECOMMUNICATIONS (BT) ENVIRONMENTAL POLICY, BT currently recovers around 1.9 million rental telephones a year for refurbishment, re-use and recycling. Making use of the return journeys of BT equipment supply vehicles, the telephones are transported from engineering service points back to central collection stores and then sent to the recycling contractor. There they are inspected and sorted, with as many as possible being recovered for re-use, the remainder being sent for materials recycling.

BT has increased the number of telephones it refurbishes, re-uses within BT or resells. During 1993/94 all telephones and answering machines recovered were sent for recycling, with none being refurbished. This is in contrast to 1996/97, when over 1.4 million telephones and answering machines were dismantled, refurbished and remanufactured to original specifications, only 450,000 being recycled.

In 1993, the cost of the recycling scheme to BT was £1.1 million (US $1.87 million). By 1997 BT had converted this loss to an income, and received £1.3 million (US$2.21 million) from the telephone recovery scheme. This contrast reflects the fact that refurbishment and re-use can be a more financially viable operation than recycling, and demonstrates the link between environmental good practice and business benefit.

Telephones and answering machines that are too badly damaged, or that are too old to be refurbished and resold, are recycled. The outer body of the telephone is made from acrylonitrile butadiene styrene (ABS). This plastic, provided it is not contaminated with other non-compatible plastics, can be granulated and reformulated. Recovered ABS from telephones is typically used in mouldings such as printer ribbon cassettes and car wheel trims. During 1996/97 BT recovered 190 tonnes of plastics from rental telephones.

The metallic content of a telephone is also recycled. Once the case has been removed, together with any other components requiring special treatment, the remainder of the telephone is granulated. Steel used in the main structural hardware is removed by electro-magnets. Coils are rich in copper, and other components such as nuts, bolts and bells are often made from brass. The edge contacts on printed circuit boards are usually coated in gold, and relay and switch contacts can be a source of other precious metals. In the same period (1996/97), over 300 kg of precious metals were recouped from telephones and answering machines.

The efficiency of the entire recycling process is dependent on the ease with which telephones can be separated into the different plastics and material types. BT is therefore investigating ways in which to improve the design of products for re-use and recycling. Materials need to be properly identified, and non-compatible plastics need to be easily separable.

Although BT prefers to refurbish and re-use where possible, where this cannot be done the current recycling process recovers over 95% by weight of the material content of telephones. The aim is to increase this through careful design and choice of materials

Box 9.6 **Case study: recycling BT telephones**

Source: BT 1997

energy-efficient household appliances. Computer manufacturers have embraced the Energy Star® initiative of the US Environmental Protection Agency (EPA), the German Blue Angel and Sweden's Good Environmental Choice eco-labels. Energy efficiency and water conservation will continue to provide challenges for designers as they seek to meet increasing community standards and tighter regulations.

Designers will also need to address the impact of their products on waste. Several forward-thinking companies are introducing design for environment (DfE) features in their products to make them easier and faster to dismantle and sort for either component re-use or materials recycling. Others are implementing viable business strategies that are based on the principles of product stewardship and product take-back.

Regulations are being introduced throughout the world to place responsibility on manufacturers for the return and re-use of EEPs. This has implications for the design of products as well as systems for repair, re-use and product take-back. In the longer term, this will change relationships between the manufacturer and their customers, with the emphasis on service rather than product.

A checklist for the design of electronic and electrical products is given in Box 9.7.

◢ Further reading

Anzovin, S., *The Green PC: Making Choices that Make a Difference* (Blue Ridge Summit, PA: McGraw–Hill, 1993).

> This book is designed to help readers find out how they can support 'green' computer manufacturers, recycle PC hardware and supplies and reduce emissions and power consumption.

Burnett Jung, L., *Designing for the Environment: A Design Guide for Information and Technology Equipment* (Washington, DC: American Plastics Council, 1995).

> This book provides some very specific guidance on the practice of design for disassembly and recyclability with a view to addressing the life-cycle environmental impacts of plastics in information technology equipment.

GE Plastics, *Design for Recycling* (Pittsfield, MA: GE Plastics, 1992).

> This is a hands-on guide to designing plastics products that can be more easily recycled. Examples described range from cars to air conditioners.

◢ Useful organisations

- Appliance Recycling Information Centre (ARIC), c/o Association of Home Appliance Manufacturers, 701 Pennsylvania Avenue, NW, Suite 900, Washington, DC 2004, USA.
- Appliance Recycling Centres of America, Inc., 7400 Excelsior Boulevard, Minneapolis, MN 55426-4517, USA.
- Industry Council for Electronic Equipment Recycling, 6 Bath Place, Rivington Street, London EC2A 3JE, UK.

Select low-impact materials (see Section 4.1)

- Avoid the use of toxic or hazardous materials
- Avoid ozone-depleting substances
- Select recycled and recyclable materials

Design for energy efficiency (see Section 4.4)

- Clarify core functions
- Look for synergies
- Aim for maximum efficiency
- Look for waste
- Design for part-load operation
- Optimise system efficiency
- Plan for ongoing improvements
- Use computer modelling

Design for durability

- Identify and eliminate potential weak points in the design, particularly for operational parts
- Ensure the product is designed for likely misuse as well the intended use
- Design for easy maintenance and repair, preferably by the owner
- Consider classic designs or other means that will encourage consumers to want to retain products for longer periods

Design for upgradability

- Design to allow new modules or functions to be added at a later date (e.g. for memory units in computers)
- Design for technical or aesthetic modularity that allows products to be renewed

Design for remanufacturing

Design for remanufacturing is similar to design for recyclability. The following principles should be followed when considering a design for possible remanufacture. The product:

- Should be 'mature' (i.e. not undergoing rapid change, in either design or materials); the products favoured for remanufacture are those with a slow rate of design from year to year
- Must be standardised and made with interchangeable parts
- Must be capable of disassembly
- Parts must be capable of repair, refurbishment or economic replacement to enable the final remanufactured product to reproduce the original performance
- Must have a 'core', which must retain a sufficient value to justify remanufacture

Box 9.7 **Design checklist for electronic and electrical products** *(continued over)*

Source: Gertsakis *et al.* 1999

Design for metal recovery

- Increase the use of metals
- Specify use of materials with recycled content
- Avoid self-contaminating combinations of materials (e.g. contamination of steel with copper can reduce the value of steel)
- Avoid toxic substances such as cadmium, asbestos and mercury that may not be accepted for shredding

Design for plastics recovery

- Minimise material variety
- Use compatible materials
- Specify materials with recycled content
- Consolidate parts
- Reduce the number of assembly operations
- Simplify and standardise component fits and interfaces
- Identify separation points between parts
- Use water-soluble adhesives where possible
- Mark materials to enhance separation

Box 9.6 (continued)

Plate 9.4 **A stockpile of power tools ready for disassembly**

Photo courtesy Robert Bosch Australia

10

DESIGNING TOMORROW TODAY

10.1 Where to from here?

The earlier chapters of this book have presented guidelines, strategies and other information for designers and product developers on how to avoid or reduce the environmental impacts of products. As an approach, design for environment (DfE) offers considerable scope and potential not only to create more benign objects but also to activate the creativity and innovation that often lies dormant among many designers and companies.

The aim has been to present a 'how to' guide for designers based on current best practice in the industry. Although acceptable over the short to medium term, DfE and the associated incremental improvements are insufficient (in isolation) as a means of achieving a sustainable future. Given the growing levels of environmental degradation around the world, few would argue that we need to take a more ambitious and longer-term view of how products are designed, manufactured, utilised and disposed of. The need for fundamental change and thinking in relation to the design process and its outcomes cannot be overstated in any discussion about sustainability.

Although business has made significant environmental advances in recent years, the rhetoric of corporate environmentalism has in many aspects outpaced its actions and outputs. In other words, conventional DfE is very much about well-intentioned tinkering, constantly shadowed by the desire to think outside the square. Sustainable products and services are imperative elements if contemporary society is to realise a more sustainable pattern of production and consumption. More importantly, the velocity at which this change must take place will have to increase dramatically over the next decade.

This final chapter highlights where and how the boundaries of DfE can be pushed. It offers some snapshots based on 'sustainable' design and not merely 'environmental' design. The prevailing message is characterised by the need for more radical strategies that maximise and enhance environmental quality and quality of life while pursuing sensible economic objectives.

10.2 Maximising eco-efficiency

A longer-term perspective suggests that DfE must be positioned in the broader framework of sustainability. The word 'sustainable' is generally used to mean the ability of the present generation to fulfil its needs without compromising the ability of future generations to fulfil their needs.[1] In practical terms, sustainability means that limits must be placed on the consumption of resources, which will in turn require policies and design strategies that produce feasible and acceptable solutions.

During the past decade, the question of sustainability has been the basis for intense debate about the need for short-term and long-term reductions in the environmental impacts of production and consumption. According to some quantitative studies, industrialised countries, with a small proportion of the world's resources, are absorbing a disproportionate quantity of resources. Von Weizsäcker *et al.* (1997), for example, point out that, with per capita consumption rates about 15 times higher in Germany than they are in India, the total ecological burden caused by 80 million people in Germany is likely to be higher than that of 900 million people in India.

The globalisation of markets is also extending the industrialised model of development (lifestyles, behaviour and consumption patterns) from industrialised countries to developing countries. What would happen if 900 million people in India used the same amount of products and services that people in Germany are using today? The planet is unlikely to be able to sustain this trend, and some resources may be depleted with potentially catastrophic consequences.

In order to avoid the risk of environmental crisis in the medium to long term, a concerted effort is required now to dramatically reduce our consumption of resources. Estimates have been made of the reduction that is required, based on different assumptions about population, average wealth per capita and metabolism (i.e. the quantity of resources used to produce a unit of product or service). On this basis, a Factor 10 or Factor 20 reduction in resource use (i.e. between 90% and 95%) is required over the next 50 years in order to provide future generations with the same resources available to us (Weterings and Opschoor, 1992).[2]

1 Such a definition is the most accepted one. It was introduced in the 'Brundtland Report' (WCED 1987).
2 The equation on which the calculation is based is

$$I = P \times W \times M$$

where I is environmental impact, P is the population, W is the average wealth per capita and M is metabolism (i.e. the quantity of resource use per unit of service), inversely proportional to eco-efficiency *(continued opposite)*.

A reduction of 90%–95% means that in 50 years time the most developed countries will need to be using only 5% of the resources they are currently using. At first glance, such a dramatic reduction seems impossible, but several studies, institutions and industrial organisations[3] suggest that this target is not impossible if the following conditions are met:

- The change should be initiated and supported by developed countries as a new model of development that could eventually be exported to developing countries.

- The change should be based not only on technological development but also on major social and cultural changes that influence production and consumption patterns.

Given the size of the reduction needed, it is clear that most of the effort to reduce energy and resource use will need to take place in the more industrialised countries. Developing countries are generally using less-efficient products and technologies, but production and consumption levels are much lower. For this reason, any limitation on consumption of resources and energy would be a limitation on their development. The challenge in the developed countries is to redesign entire production and consumption systems in order to produce, in the medium to long term, the same level of wellbeing and the same quality of life with less resources and energy.

The challenge of sustainability is already providing an incentive to develop more innovative policies and design strategies. Developments in technology are providing significant opportunities for change, but new visions are also needed to achieve more fundamental technological, social, cultural and economic shifts. Designers will play an essential role in shaping a more sustainable future. This role will include incremental improvements to the design of products as well as the development of a completely new generation of products and services.

The calculations are based on different projections of population growth and average wealth per capita in 50 years' time, with the target being not to increase or reduce the environmental impact. The variable in the equation is the metabolism. For instance, if in 50 years' time the population doubles (from p to $2p$) and the average wealth per capita increases fivefold (from w to $5w$), the metabolism has to be reduced tenfold (from $10m$ to m) in order to keep to the present value of environmental impact. That is,

$$p \times w \times 10m = 2p \times 5w \times m$$

3 See Jansen (1994, 1997, 1998) and von Weizsäcker et al. (1997). One of the most relevant institutional initiatives has been undertaken by the Dutch government and has generated several publications (e.g. VROM 1993a, 1993b; Jansen et al. 1998). On the industrial front, the World Business Council for Sustainable Development, including major multinational companies, was created soon after the 1992 Rio Earth Summit for the development of profitable business strategies that preserve environmental sustainability. Most of these organisations also refer to the Carnoules Declaration (Factor 10 Club 1994) issued by a group of major institutional and industrial representatives (the Factor 10 Club).

Incremental changes in technology are continuously improving the eco-effi-ciency of products and services. Some sectors, such as that of domestic appliances and vehicles, have been under pressure for some time to reduce energy consumption. A recent study in Australia has demonstrated that, if consumers were encouraged to use the most efficient household appliances currently on the market, the result would be a reduction in energy and water consumption and associated greenhouse gas emissions of 50%–70% (i.e. a factor of 2 to 3; Morelli 1999b). Governments could encourage this shift (e.g. through price rebates and product bounties that remove older, inefficient products from operation).

Many authors, however, express doubts about the ability of technology alone to deliver the Factor 10 or 20 reduction needed for long-term sustainability (e.g. Jansen 1994; Manzini 1997). They argue that the shift to sustainability will also require significant cultural changes. In this sense the challenge of sustainability requires a shift from the eco-redesign of existing products to solutions that are, at present, beyond our technological and cultural horizons.

10.3 Beyond the ecological horizon

New materials and technologies have the potential to significantly improve the eco-efficiency of products. The evolution of polymeric materials, for example, is generating new products that are lighter and stronger. The increasing percentage of polymers in cars is contributing to a reduction in fuel consumption. The use of plastics instead of heavier materials in other products, such as packaging and appliances, is reducing overall weight and therefore the environmental impacts of transport.

A variety of alternative energy technologies are being developed. Electric energy is a valid substitute for oil in the automotive industry and has the potential to greatly reduce air pollution. Electric cars are still in the developmental stage, however. Other sources of energy being developed include hydrogen and solar power. Other technologies being developed to improve energy efficiency include ultrasonic clothes-washers and dishwashers, new refrigeration systems and intelligent electronic controls. A significant leap forward in technology will depend, however, on:

- The integration of different technological innovations
- The application of new technologies on a large scale (e.g. to traffic systems, buildings and to domestic and office products)

In the automotive industry, for example, the use of super-light polymeric materials would certainly increase the efficiency of electric or hybrid engines, and electronic controls would reduce the dispersion of energy in the transmission parts. Prototypes of super-efficient products have been proposed by many automotive companies, and the application of such innovation would benefit from the creation of economies of scale.

Information technology (IT) is also expected to contribute to a large reduction in environmental impacts, for it allows for better control and co-ordination of energy and resource use. The creation of information networks is expected to improve transportation systems, especially in the larger cities. More advanced vehicles are already provided with navigation systems that provide direction on the optimal route from A to B. IT is expected to contribute to a radical change in work practices that could reduce the need for physical transportation, particularly during peak-hour movements.[4]

In other sectors, IT is expected to integrate and optimise large systems such as domestic and office systems. Computerised domestic control systems will decide autonomously when and how to use domestic appliances and will co-ordinate the use of energy; for example, water and air heaters will be able to use waste heat from the refrigerator. The use of special polymers in windows will improve energy efficiency by optimising the penetration of light and by reducing the dispersion of heat in domestic and office buildings.

The concept of 'industrial ecology' is useful in helping us to understand how we might be able to reshape modern industrial systems to resemble natural systems. In natural systems, nothing is wasted. Energy and materials disposed of by certain organisms are a resource for other organisms. The application of this concept to industrial systems would mean that waste from production in one process would be re-used or consumed in another process. IT would provide self-regulating mechanisms for optimising the use of resources and energy.

10.4 Beyond the cultural horizon

Increasing competition in the global market is forcing companies to increase the value of their products by adding a greater service component. Several companies already offer maintenance, assistance and product take-back as value-added features to their services and products. This trend is increasing the relevance of information, communication and knowledge-related product values relative to their physical appearance. Products are often thrown away because they have lost their social and cultural attractiveness, even if they are still in perfect working order. The answer may be to move away from consumer ownership of products and to focus more on the service or 'utilisation value' that is provided by products.

If products are quickly used and thrown away it is reasonable to think of solutions that are no longer based on ownership. These could include leasing or

4   The use of information technology is expected to increase the phenomenon of telework and to reduce the number of trips to work. Such a reduction has been predicted for a long time, but to date has never really happened. In fact, the independence of work from geographic location is insufficient for a wide diffusion of telework. For an extensive analysis of the contribution of information technology to the diffusion of telework and to the reduction of physical transportation in metropolitan and regional areas, see Morelli 1999a.

renting products from the producer or an authorised leasing agency instead of buying them. This would reduce the amount of wasted resources, because consumers would use the product only for the time they needed it, and the manufacturer or agency would retain ownership. The leasing agency would also have an interest in maintaining the product in good working order and in extending its life as long as possible. At the end of the product's life, recycling would be easier as the leaser would have control of the take-back system.

From industry's point of view, such a cultural change would imply a shift in emphasis away from production and towards consumer satisfaction and quality. This is what Stahel (1994, 1997) defines as the service economy. Tailor-made products, such as office systems, would be designed for defined utilisation periods; replacement and updating would guarantee resource productivity. The success of companies such as Xerox and Interface (Box 10.1) that have adopted strategies based on this philosophy is expected to encourage similar initiatives by other companies.

THE EVERGREEN PROGRAMME, DEVELOPED BY INTERFACE FLOORING SYSTEMS INC., provides a new approach to the conventional sale of carpet. Through this programme, commercial and institutional customers lease the services of replaceable carpet tiles (offering functionality, colour, design and aesthetics) without having to take responsibility for disposal when they become worn. Instead of buying and replacing entire flooring systems every few years, customers prolong the life of the flooring by replacing individual tiles as needed.

The programme provides a complete service package that includes design layouts, product selection, carpet, access flooring, furniture lifting, installation, ongoing maintenance and ultimate removal for reclamation or recycling. Interface Flooring Systems assumes responsibility for the on-site condition of the carpet and for its eventual disposal and re-use in ways that do not harm the environment (e.g. old carpet tiles can be ground into a powder that can then be moulded into new products or used as backing materials). Through the Evergreen programme, Interface is drastically dematerialising its industrial process while also saving customers money and protecting the environment.

Box 10.1 **Case study: the Evergreen programme**

Source: PCSD 1997

From the consumer's perspective, the emphasis on utilisation value would also require a cultural shift to increase the acceptability of leasing arrangements. Leasing or renting is particularly attractive for resource-intensive products such as appliances and cars. Car sharing is one example of how consumers might be able to reduce the environmental impacts of transport while saving money and improving quality of life (Box 10.2). In developed countries, a large percentage of cars travelling in urban areas are used by a single passenger. Car sharing would increase the intensity of utilisation of cars while reducing the stress of driving.

The shift to a service economy based on utilisation value rather than ownership would encourage the development of new products with lower material content but with greater emphasis on customer service. In this sense the service

SWISS MEMBERSHIP OF CAR-SHARING SCHEMES HAS GROWN EXPONENTIALLY over the past 10 years, reaching over 12,000 in 1996 and increasing by about 50%–75% per year. Early members were environmentally motivated, but more recent members are choosing to car-share for convenience or to save money. Car sharers drive less than do car owners because they do not have a car in their garage or on the doorstep that they can use for short trips. Former car owners who join the system drive less than they did before (down from an average of 9,000 km per year to 4,000 km per year) but no longer borrow or hire cars. Those joining the system report an improved quality of life, with more flexibility in their personal mobility and less stress from city driving and car ownership.

Box 10.2 **Case study: car-sharing schemes in Switzerland**

Source: OECD 1998

economy can be seen as the first step towards a dematerialised society. Dematerialisation implies a highly intelligent production and consumption system in which knowledge-based services will successfully compete with resource-intensive products and services. For example, telecommunications will be a reliable and attractive alternative to transport systems. Working at home or in residential areas will be more attractive than travelling to work in the city and video-conferencing will be preferred to overseas business trips.

10.5 Conclusions

There is little doubt that sustainability will require an evolutionary change in the way we conceive, design, manufacture and consume products. This will involve complex interactions between technological innovation and evolving socio-economic and cultural systems. The role of designers in this process is a very important one. Although the ability of designers to force change, either through legislation or moral argument, is limited, they can propose innovative solutions that provide a way forward, both through visualising future scenarios and through stimulating greater innovation.

Design strategies in pursuit of sustainability could include:

- Increasing the range of alternatives (i.e. the set of 'solution strategies' for an environmental problem; such strategies have to be technically and economically feasible)

- Promoting consumers' ability to find their own solutions to problems (i.e consumers have to be given the chance to use and/or misuse products, without making irreparable mistakes that might have dangerous environmental consequences)[5]

---

5   One of the major problems with modern technology is that the high level of specialisation of certain technological products and processes does not allow for errors. In

- Stimulating the collective imagination (i.e. the collective ability to 'see' solutions that are still not clearly expressed); the designer can operate at the level of cultural values, quality criteria and visions of 'future worlds' in order to drive the demand for products and services generated by such values

Designers are at the significant point of conjunction between technological and cultural worlds. They are therefore in a privileged position to capture and act on signals for change. The future challenge for designers is to understand the critical role they play in shaping our future and to use this ability and skill set to move design into a more sustainable future. As reinforced throughout this book, there are few human endeavours that possess design's unique potential to 'lock in' positive socio-environmental qualities. Creating outcomes that are environmentally necessary, socially desirable, culturally acceptable and economically appropriate directly reflect the designer's job description—challenging, realistic and timely.

large systems (such as computer systems, nuclear power plants, traffic control systems) the lack of *error-friendliness* can cause catastrophes, as the systems are not able to respond to users' mistakes. Also, on a smaller scales, such as in everyday products, high technological specialisation may create problems in coping with errors. Most people have experienced a sense of helplessness in trying to repair simple faults in a modern car or photocopier.

REFERENCES

ACA (Australian Consumers Association) (1992) 'Why Waste Energy?', *Choice*, May 1992: 12-16.

ACA (Australian Consumers Association) (1993) 'Disposable Appliances', *Choice*, October 1993: 16-17.

Ackerman, F. (1997) *Why Do We Recycle?* (Washington, DC: Island Press).

Ahbe, S., A. Braunschweig and R. Mueller-Wenk (1990) *Methodik für Oekobikanzen (Method for Ecobalance)* (publication 133; Bern: BUWAL).

Anderson, P., S. Kelly and T. Rattray (1995) 'Redesigning for Recycling', *BioCycle*, July 1995: 64-65.

Antonides, G. (1990) *The Life-time of a Durable Good: An Economic Psychological Approach. Theory and Decision Library*. Volume 12, Series A. *Philosophy and Methodology of the Social Sciences* (Dordrecht, Netherlands: Kluwer Academic Publishers).

Aplin, G., P. Beggs, G. Brierley, H. Cleugh, P. Curson, P. Mitchell, A. Pitman and D. Rich (1999) *Global Environmental Crises: An Australian Perspective* (Melbourne: Oxford University Press, 2nd edn).

Baillon, J., and J.P. Ceron (n.d.) *Durabilité des Biens et Gestion de l'Environnement* (Paris: Ministère de la Qualité de la Vie).

BIEC (Beverage Industry Environment Council) (1998) *Recycling Audit and Garbage Bin Analysis* (Melbourne: BIEC).

BIEC (Beverage Industry Environment Council) (2000) *Recycling Guide for Beverage and Food Manufacturers Marketing in PET Containers* (Sydney: BIEC).

BLS (US Bureau of Labor Statistics) (1974) *Handbook of Labor Statistics* (Washington, DC: BLS).

Boehm, K., and T. Hunt Jr (1995) 'Florida's Advance Disposal Fee: Success or Failure?', *Warmer Bulletin, World Resource Foundation, UK* 46 (August 1995): 12-13.

Boustead, I. (1993) *Eco-profiles of the European Plastics Industry. Report 3. Polyethylene and Polypropylene* (Brussels: European Centre for Plastics in the Environment).

Boustead, I. (1994) *Eco-profiles of the European Plastics Industry. Report 4. Polystyrene* (Brussels: European Centre for Plastics in the Environment).

Boyden, S., M. Common, S. Dovers and E. Madsden (1991) *A Comparative Environmental Study of Packaging Alternatives for Liquid-food Products* (report to the Association of Liquidpaperboard Carton Manufacturers; Canberra: Centre for Policy Studies, Australian National University).

Brezet J.C., and C.G. van Hemel (1997) *Ecodesign: A Promising Approach to Sustainable Production and Consumption* (Paris: United Nations Environment Programme).

BT (British Telecommunications plc) (1997) *BT Environment Report 1997* (London: BT, www.bt.com/world/environment).

Butlin, J. (1982) *Product Durability and Product Life Extension: Their Contribution to Solid Waste* (Paris: Organisation for Economic Co-operation and Development).

Canon (1993) *The Canon Story 1993/94* (Tokyo: Canon Inc).

CEPA (Commonwealth Environment Protection Agency) (1996) 'The Montreal Protocol on Substances that Deplete the Ozone Layer' (fact sheet; Canberra: CEPA).

Chouinard, Y., and M. Brown (1997) 'Going Organic: Converting Patagonia's Cotton Product Line', *Journal of Industrial Ecology* 1.1: 117-29.

CMI (Centre of Environmental Science) (1995) *Beginning LCA: A Guide into Life Cycle Assessment* (Leiden, Netherlands: CMI, Leiden University, www.leidenuniv.nl/interfac/cml/index.html).

Collins, P. (1995) *Dictionary of Ecology and the Environment* (Teddington, UK: Peter Collins Publishing, 3rd edn).

Collis, B. (1999) 'A Quiet Revolutionary Hopes to Pack a Punch', *The Age*, 13 June 1999: 18.

Cooper (1990) *Are Textiles Finishing the Environment?* (Manchester, UK: Textiles Institute).

Cramer, J. (1993) *Government Policies to Promote Cleaner Production in the Netherlands* (Apeldoorn, Netherlands: TNO Centre for Technology and Policy Studies).

Davis, A.G. (1995) 'Extended Producer Responsibility: A New Principle for a New Generation of Pollution Prevention', in *Proceedings of the Symposium on Extended Producer Responsibility*, Washington, DC, 14-15 November 1994 (Knoxville, TN: Center for Clean Products and Clean Technologies).

DesignTex (n.d.) 'The William McDonough Fabric Collection', media release, DesignTex, New York.

Dickinson, G. (1997) *Life Cycle Assessment (LCA) and Textile Design with Reference to Textile Dyes*, address to EcoReDesign™ Seminar, Centre for Design, Royal Melbourne Institute of Technology, Melbourne, Australia, 5 September 1997.

Dormer, P. (1992) *Design Since 1945: World of Art* (London: Thames & Hudson).

ECMA (European Association for Standardising Information and Communication Systems) (1997) *Product-Related Environmental Attributes* (technical report TR/70; Geneva: ECMA).

EcoRecycle Victoria (n.d.) Information Sheets (Melbourne: EcoRecycle Victoria).

EGEA (Electrolux Group Environmental Affairs) (1997) *Annual Environmental Report* (Stockholm: Electrolux).

ENDS (Environmental Data Services) (1992) 'Electronics Waste Recycling Gathers Momentum', *ENDS Report* 215 (December 1992): 1192.

ENDS (Environmental Data Services) (1996a) 'SmithKline Beecham: Integrating LCA into Packaging and Product Development', *ENDS Report* 255 (April 1996): 22-25.

ENDS (Environmental Data Services) (1996b) *ENDS Report* 258 (July 1996): 18-20.

EPA (US Environmental Protection Agency) (1995) *An Introduction to Environmental Accounting as a Business Management Tool: Key Concepts and Terms* (publication 742-R-95-001; Washington, DC: EPA).

Epton, M. (1997) Untitled presentation to *Textiles and the Environment* seminar, Royal Melbourne Institute of Technology, Melbourne, Australia, 5 September 1997.

Factor 10 Club (1994) *Carnoules Declaration* (Wuppertal, Germany: Wuppertal Institute).

FCPAN (Fibre Council and Pesticide Action Network) (1999), *Organic Cotton Directory 1998-99* (Greenfield, MA: FCPAN, Organic Trade Association).

Firth, D. (1993) 'Survey Reveals the "True" Cost of Notebook PCs', *The Age Green Guide*, 18 November 1993: 27.

FoE (Friends of the Earth) (1996) *The Good Wood Guide* (Melbourne: Friends of the Earth).

Fox, B. (1993) 'Green TV Law Stores up Mountain of Trouble', *New Scientist*, 4 September 1993: 20.

Fox, B. (1998) 'Stand by for Savings', *New Scientist* 159.2142 (July 1998): 7.

Franklin Associates (1999) *Characterisation of Municipal Solid Waste in the United States: 1998 Update, Executive Summary* (Washington, DC: US Environmental Protection Agency).

GE Plastics (1992) *Design for Recycling* (Pittsfield, MA: GE Plastics).

Gertsakis J., H. Lewis and C. Ryan (1997) *A Guide to EcoReDesign™* (Melbourne: Centre for Design, Royal Melbourne Institute of Technology).

Gertsakis J., S. Reardon and A. Sweatman (1999) *Appliance Reuse and Recycling: A Product Stewardship Guide* (Melbourne: Centre for Design, Royal Melbourne Institute of Technology).

Goedkoop, M. (1995) *De Eco-indicator 95* (final report, NOH Report 9523; Amersfoort, Netherlands: PRé Consultants).

Goedkoop, M., and R. Spriensma (1999) *The Eco-indicator 99: A Damage Oriented Method for Life Cycle Impact Assessment Methodology Report* (Amersfoort, Netherlands: PRé Consultants).

Graedel, T.E., and B.R. Allenby (1995) *Industrial Ecology* (Englewood Cliffs, NJ: Prentice–Hall).

Grant, T., and H. Lewis (1997a) *Strategies for Reducing Plastics Waste: Report to the Plastics and Chemicals Industries Association* (Melbourne: Centre for Design, Royal Melbourne Institute of Technology).

Grant, T., and H. Lewis (1997b) *Sustainable Packaging: Beyond Recycling* (EcoReDesign™ Supplement; Melbourne: Centre for Design, Royal Melbourne Institute of Technology).

Greene, D. (1992) *Life Cycle Analysis of Washing Machines* (Sydney: Australian Consumers Association).

Greig-Gran, M., S. Bass, J. Bishop, S. Roberts, N. Robins, R. Sandbrook, M. Bazett, V. Gadvi and S. Subak (1998) 'Towards a Sustainable Paper Cycle: A Summary', *Journal of Industrial Ecology* 1.3: 47-68.

Grose, L. (1995) 'The Cotton Chain', *Pesticides News* 28 (June 1995): 9-11.

Hakim, D. (1995) 'A Fashionable Joint Venture', *The Washington Post*, 31 May 1995, www.fornits.com/curiosity/hemp/washpost.htm.

Handspring (1999) *Springboard White Paper* (Mountain View, CA: Handspring).

Henstock, M.E. (1988) *Design for Recyclability* (London: The Institute of Metals).

Herman Miller (1993) *Environmental Initiatives Brochure* (Zeeland, Netherlands: Herman Miller).

Hicks, C. (1994) 'The Role of Ecodesign', in *Ecodesign in the Telecommunications Industry* (Royal Society for the Arts [RSA] Papers; London: RSA, with British Telecommunications plc).

Hill, S. (1997) 'Cars that Grow on Trees', *New Scientist*, 1 February 1997.

Hunt, M. (1991) 'Back to the Future', *Materials Engineering*, July 1991: 21-24.

Industry Commission (1996) *Packaging and Labelling* (Melbourne: Industry Commission).

Interface (1996) *Annual Report* (Atlanta, GA: Interface Inc.).

ISO (International Organisation for Standardisation (2000) *ISO/DIS 11469. Plastics: Generic Information and Marking of Plastic Parts* (Geneva: ISO).

Jansen, J.L.A. (1994) 'Towards a Sustainable Future: En Route with Technology!', in Dutch Committee for Long-Term Environmental Policy (ed.), *The Environment: Towards a Sustainable Future* (Dordrecht, Netherlands: Kluwer Academic Publishers).

Jansen, J.L.A. (1997) 'Sustainable Development: A Challenge for Material Technology', *Proceedings of the 5th European Conference on Advanced Materials and Processes and Applications* 4 (21–23 April 1997): 303-11.

Jansen, J.L.A. (1998) 'The Challenge for Technology', keynote paper presented at the ENVENT Summit, Melbourne, 10 December 1998, http://envent.rmit.edu.au/summit/jansen.pdf.

Jansen, J.L.A., C. Bakker, H. Bouwmeester, T. Kievid, G. Van Grotveld and P. Vergragt (1998) *STD Vision 2040–1998: Technology, Key to Sustainable Prosperity* (The Hague: ten Hagen & Stam).

Johnston, M.W. (1993) 'Taking the Byte Out of Electronic Waste', *Tomorrow* 2 (April–June 1993): 10-13.

Jones, J. (1997) *Cost and Material Savings from Reusable Transport Packaging* (presentation to EcoReDesign™ Seminar, Sydney; Melbourne, Australia: Centre for Design, Royal Melbourne Institute of Technology).

Kodak (1997) *Health, Safety and Environment: 1997 Corporate Annual Report* (Rochester, NY: Kodak, www.kodak.com).

Kramer, J., and M. Ferstera (1995) *Wilkhahn Green: A Company in the Process of Change* (Bad Munder, Germany: Wilkhahn, Wilkening & Hahne).

Kuraska, H. (1995) 'Extended Producer Responsibility in Asia', in *Proceedings of the Symposium on Extended Producer Responsibility*, Washington, DC, June 1995 (Knoxville, TN: University of Tennessee): 95-109.

Leaversuch, R.D. (1991) 'Chemical Recycling Brings Real Versatility to Solid-waste Management', *Modern Plastics International*, July 1991: 26.

Lehmer, A., and M. Marden (n.d.) 'Kenaf: The Clean Paper Crop', www.rethinkpaper.org/content/content.cfm?pagename=solutions.

Lehmer, A., B. West and S. Chamberlain (n.d.) 'Hemp: The Hardy Paper Crop', *ReThink Paper*, www.rethinkpaper.org/content/content.cfm?pagename=solutions.

Lifset, R.J. (1995) 'Extending Producer Responsibility in North America: Progress, Pitfalls and Prospects in 1990s', *Proceedings of the Symposium on Extended Producer Responsibility*, Washington, DC, June 1995 (Knoxville, TN: University of Tennessee).

Lowe, S. (1993) 'Study of Top-Selling Portables Reveals Long-Term Costs', *The Age*, 16 November 1993: 25.

LRRA (Litter Research and Recycling Association) (1996) *Recycling Audit and Garbage Bin Analysis* (Melbourne: LRRA).

Lund, R.T. (1975) *Incentives for Longer Product Life: A Case Study* (working paper CPA/WPA-75-15; Cambridge, MA: Centre for Policy Alternatives, Massachusetts Institute of Technology).

Lund, R.T. (1984) 'Remanufacturing', *Technology Review*, February/March 1984: 18-29.

McDonough, W. (1993) 'Design, Ecology, Ethics and the Making of Things', Centennial sermon at the Cathedral of St John the Divine, New York City, 7 February 1993.

McLaren, W (1995) 'Wear it, write on it', *Object* 3-4: 36.

Makower, J. (1993) 'A Current Affair: The New Generation of Energy-efficient, Earth-friendly Appliances', *The Greenconsumer Letter*, October 1993: 6.

Manzini, E. (1997) 'Designing Sustainability Leapfrog: Application of a Possible Future', *Domus* 789 (January 1997)..

Marquardt, S. (n.d.) 'Pick Your Cotton', *EcoMall*, www.ecomall.com/greenshopping/mpick.htm.

May, A. (1995) 'What's a Girl Got to Do?', *Patagonia Globe*, November 1995: 3.

MCC (Micro Computer Corporation) (1993) *Environmental Consciousness: A Strategic Consciousness Issue for the Electronics and Computer Industry* (Dallas, TX: MCC).

Meadows, D., D. Meadows, J. Randers and W. Behrens (1972) *The Limits to Growth* (London: Pan).

Meikle, J. (1995) *American Plastics: A Cultural History* (New Brunswick, NJ: Rutgers University Press).

Morelli, N. (1999a) 'The Space of Telework: Physical and Virtual Future Configurations for Remote Work', *Foresight* 1.3: 229-42.

Morelli, N. (1999b) 'Technological Innovation and Resource Efficiency: A Model for Australian Household Appliances', *Journal of Sustainable Product Design*.

Nader, R. (1965) *Unsafe at Any Speed* (New York: Grossman).

Neutra R. (1954) *Survival through Design* (New York: Oxford University Press).

Nokia (1999) *Nokia Environmental Report* (Espoo, Finland: Nokia).

Norwegian Ministry of Environment (1996) *Green Goods: The Third International Conference on Product Oriented Environmental Policy*, Oslo, 15–17 February 1996.

OECD (Organisation for Economic Co-operation and Development) (1993) *Applying Economic Instruments to Packaging Waste: Practical Issues for Product Charges and Deposit–Refund Systems* (Monograph 82; Paris: OECD).

OECD (Organisation for Economic Co-operation and Development) (1996) *Pollution Prevention and Control: Extended Producer Responsibility in the OECD Area: Phase 1 Report* (Paris: OECD).

OECD (Organisation for Economic Co-operation and Development) (1997) *Extended Producer Responsibility: Case Study on German Packaging Ordinance* (Paris: OECD).

OECD (Organisation for Economic Co-operation and Development) (1998) *Ecoefficiency* (Paris: OECD).

OTA (US Office of Technology Assessment, US Congress) (1992) *Green Products by Design: Choices for a Cleaner Environment* (OTA-E-5451; Washington, DC: US Government Printing Office).

Paakkunainen, R. (1995) *Textiles and the Environment* (Eindhoven, Netherlands: European Design Centre).

Packaging Council of Australia (n.d.) *The National Packaging Covenant*, www.packcoun. com.au.

Packard, V. (1956) *The Hidden Persuaders* (Harmondsworth, UK: Penguin Books).

Packard, V. (1961) *The Waste-Makers: A Startling Revelation of Planned Wastefulness and Obsolescence in Industry Today* (London: Longman).

Papanek, P. (1971) *Design for the Real World: Human Ecology and Social Change* (New York: Pantheon Books).

Papanek, P. (1995) *The Green Imperative: Ecology and Ethics in Design and Architecture* (London: Thames & Hudson).

Patagonia (1995) *Organic Cotton Story* (Ventura, CA: Patagonia).

Pawley, M. (1990) *Design Heroes: Buckminster Fuller* (London: Grafton).

PCSD (President's Council on Sustainable Development) (1997) *The Road to Sustainable Development: A Snapshot of Activities in the United States*, http://clinton2.nara.gov/ PCSD/Publications/Snapshot.html.

Pears, A. (1997) *Global Warming: Cool It! A Home Guide to Reducing Energy Costs and Greenhouse Gases* (Canberra: Environment Australia).

PIA (Plastics Institute of America) (1983) *Research Report: Shredder Residuals* (Lowell, MA: PIA).

Rathje, W. (1992) *Rubbish!* (New York: HarperCollins).

Raymond Communications (2000) *Guide to Recycling Laws: Country-by-Country Summaries. A14–A22* (College Park, MD: Raymond Communications).

Redd, A. (1992) 'World's First Automobile Disassembly Plant', *BioCycle*, February 1992: 82-83.

Saphire, D. (1994) *Delivering the Goods: Benefits of Reusable Shipping Containers* (New York: Inform).

Schmidt-Bleek, F. (1998) *MAIA: An introduction into the Material Intensity Analysis following the MIPS concept* (Wuppertal, Germany: Wuppertal Institute).

SETAC (Society of Environmental Toxicology and Chemistry) (1992) *Life Cycle Assessment Data Quality: A Technical Framework* (Washington, DC: SETAC).

SimsMetal (1991) *Plastics Recycling: Review of SimsMetal* (Sydney: SimsMetal, www. simsmetal.com.au).

Sloan, C. (1998) 'Toltec Recycles Fabric Fiber', *Home Textiles Today*, 13 April 1998: 14.

SmithKline Beecham (1998) *SmithKline Beecham Environment and Safety Report 1998*, www.sb.com/company/esr/1998/04stew.htm.

SRD (Society for Responsible Design) (1997) 'Responsible Apparel Design', *Loose Threads* (July 1997, Sydney, www.green.net.au/srd).

SRI (Steel Recycling Institute) (n.d.) *Steel Recycling Starts in the Home*, www.recyclesteel.org/fact/index.html.

Stahel, W.R. (1994) 'The Utilisation-Focused Service Economy: Resource Efficiency and Product-Life Extension', in B.R. Allenby and D. Richards (eds.), *The Greening of Industrial Ecosystems* (Washington, DC: National Academy Press).

Stahel, W.R. (1997) *The Functional Economy: Cultural and Organizational Change* (Washington, DC: National Academy Press).

Steelcase (1993) *Built to be Rebuilt, Steelcase: An Environmental Partnership* (corporate environmental statement; Grand Rapids, MI: Steelcase).

Steen, B., and S. O'Ryding (1991) *The EPS Environmental Accounting Method: An Application of Environmental Accounting Principles for Evaluation and Valuation of Environmental Impact in Product Design* (Gothenburg: Swedish Environmental Research Institute).

Strong, G. (1998) 'How is the air up there?' *The Age*, 29 April 1998: 15.

Sustainable Solutions (1993) *Greenhouse Saving Office Equipment* (Melbourne: Victoria Environment Protection Agency).

Sweatman, A., C. Chew, S. Wang, D. Tsuda and R. Aver (2000) 'Design for Environment: A Case Study of the Power Mac G4 Desktop Computer', *International Symposium on Electronics and the Environment, 2000* (San Francisco, CA: IEEE).

Taschen, B. (1993) *Package Design in Japan* (Cologne: Benedikt Taschen).

Teitenberg, T. (1988) *Environmental and Natural Resource Economics* (Glenview, IL: Scott, Foresman).

Tellus Institute (1992) *CSG/Tellus Packaging Study, Volume 1* (prepared for the Council of State Governments [CSG] and the US Environmental Protection Agency; Boston, MA: Tellus Institute).

Tomlinson, J.J., and D.T. Rizy (1998) *Bern Clothes Washer Study Final Report* (Washington, DC: US Department of Energy).

Treloar, G.J. (1994) *Energy Analysis of the Construction of Office Buildings* (masters dissertation; Geelong, Australia: Deakin University).

Tuohy, W. (1993) 'Pare Excellence', *The Age*, 30 October 1993 (extra): 12.

UNEP (United Nations Environment Programme) (1996) *Life Cycle Assessment: What it is and How to do It* (Nairobi: UNEP, www.unep.org).

UNEP (United Nations Environment Programme) (1997) *Global State of the Environment Report 1997* (Global Environment Outlook-1; New York: Oxford University Press).

UNEP (United Nations Environment Programme)/TU Delft/Rathenau Institute (1997) *Eco-Design: A Promising Approach to Sustainable Production and Consumption* (Stevenage, UK: EarthPrint, www.earthprint.com).

VEPA (Victoria Environment Protection Authority) (1997) *Cleaner Production Case Studies* (publication 536, July 1997; Melbourne: VEPA).

VEPA (Victoria Environment Protection Authority) (1998) *Regulatory Impact Statement: Environment Protection (Prescribed Waste) Regulations* (publication 613; Melbourne: VEPA).

von Weizsäcker, E.U., A. Lovins and L.H. Lovins (1997) *Factor Four: Doubling Wealth, Halving Resource Use* (Sydney: Allen & Unwin).

VROM (Ministerie van Volkshuisvesting, Ruimtelijke Ordening en Milieubehher, Netherlands) (1993a) *The Best of Both Worlds: Sustainability and Quality Lifestyles in the 21st Century* (Oxford, UK: Environmental Resource Limited).

VROM (Ministerie van Volkshuisvesting, Ruimtelijke Ordening en Milieubehher, Netherlands) (1993b) *Every Decision Counts: Consumer Choices and Environmental Impacts* (Oxford, UK: Environmental Resource Limited).

Wackernagel, M. (1997) *Ecological Footprints of Nations* (San José, Costa Rica: Earth Council).

Walsh, J., and M. Brown (1995) 'Pricing Environmental Impacts: A Tale of Two T-shirts', *illahee* 11.3–4: 175-82.

WCED (World Commission on Environment and Development) (1987) *Our Common Future* (Oxford, UK: Oxford University Press).

Webb, C. (1997) 'Smarter sleeker op shops buy into the recycling revolution', *The Age*, 15 June 1997: 7.

Weidema, B.P. (1998) *Environmental Assessment of Products: A Textbook on Life Cycle Assessment* (Helsinki: Finnish Association of Graduate Engineers [TEK], 3rd edn).

Weterings, R.A.P.M., and J.B. Opschoor (1992) *The Eco-capacity as a Challenge to Technological Development* (Rijswijk, Netherlands: Advisory Council for Research on Nature and Environment).

Whitely, N. (1993) *Design for Society* (London: Reaktion Books).

Wood, C. (1992) 'Plastic Possibilities', *Design World* 23: 16-27.

WRI (World Resources Institute) (1998) *World Resources 1998/99* (Oxford, UK: Oxford University Press).

Wright, B. (1993) 'From the Sheep's Back', *Rural Research* 159 (Winter 1993): 9-11.

ABBREVIATIONS

ABS	acrylonitrile butadiene styrene
ACA	Australian Consumers Association
APME	Association of Plastic Manufacturers in Europe
ARIC	Appliance Recycling Information Centre
BLS	US Bureau of Labor Statistics
BOD	biochemical oxygen demand
BT	British Telecommunications
BUWAL	Bundesamt für Umwelt, Wald und Landschaft (Swiss Environment Agency)
CCA	Coca-Cola Amatil
CFC	chlorofluorocarbon
Cl_2	chlorine
CML	Centre for Environmental Science, Leiden University, Netherlands
CO	carbon monoxide
CO_2	carbon dioxide
COD	chemical oxygen demand
CRC	Co-operative Research Centre
CSIRO	Commonwealth Scientific and Industrial Research Organisation
C_xH_y	hydrocarbon
DALY	disability adjusted life years
DfE	design for environment
DOE	US Department of Energy
DSD	Duales System Deutschland
ECF	elemental chlorine-free
ECMA	European Association for Standardising Information and Communication Systems
EEA	European Environment Agency
EEP	electronic and electrical product
EI99	Eco-indicator 99
ENDS	Environmental Data Services
EPA	US Environmental Protection Agency
EPR	extended producer responsibility
EPS	environmental priority strategies
EPS	expanded polystyrene
EVA	ethylene vinyl acetate
EVOH	ethylene vinyl alcohol
FAO	Food and Agricultural Organisation of the United Nations
FCPAN	Fibre Council and Pesticide Action Network
FMEA	failure mode and effect analysis
FoE	Friends of the Earth
FSC	Forest Stewardship Council
GDP	gross domestic product
GPA	general product analysis
H_2S	sulphide
HCFC	hydrochlorofluorocarbon
HDPE	high-density polyethylene
HFC	hydrofluorocarbon

ICC	International Chamber of Commerce
ICT	information and communications technology
ISO	International Organisation for Standardisation
IT	information technology
LCA	life-cycle assessment
LDPE	low-density polyethylene
LLDPE	linear low-density polyethylene
LRRA	Litter Research and Recycling Association
MCC	Micro Computer Corporation
MDF	medium-density fibreboard
MECO	materials–energy–chemicals–other
MIPS	material input per unit of service
N_2O	nitrous oxide
NGO	non-governmental organisation
NH_3	ammonia
NiCd	nickel–cadmium
NiMH	nickel metal hydride
NO_2	nitrogen dioxide
NO_3	nitrogen trioxide
NO_x	nitrogen oxides
OECD	Organisation for Economic Co-operation and Development
OEM	original equipment manufacturer
OTA	US Office of Technology Assessment
PAF	percentage affected fraction
PAH	polycyclic aromatic hydrocarbon
PCB	polychlorinated biphenyl
PCT	polychlorinated triphenyl
PE	polyethylene
PET	polyethylene terephthalate
PIA	Plastics Institute of America
PO_4	phosphate
PO_x	phosphates (PO_3, PO_4)
PP	polypropylene
PS	polystyrene
PVC	polyvinyl chloride
PVDC	polyvinylidene chloride
R&D	research and development
RMIT	Royal Melbourne Institute of Technology
SCP	Sustainable Cotton Project
SETAC	Society for Environmental Toxicology and Chemistry
SO_2	sulphur dioxide
SO_x	sulphur oxides
SOCOG	Sydney Organising Committee for the Olympic Games
SPI	Society of the Plastics Industry
SPM	suspended particulate matter
SRI	Steel Recycling Institute
TCF	totally chlorine-free
TEN	Textiles Environmental Network
THC	tetrahydrocannabinol
TNO	Netherlands Organisation for Applied Scientific Research
TU Delft	Technical Universities of Delft
UNEP	United Nations Environment Programme
VCM	vinyl chloride monomer
VEPA	Victoria Environment Protection Authority
VOC	volatile organic compound
VROM	Ministerie van Volkshuisvesting, Ruimtelijke Ordening en Milieubehher (Netherlands Ministry for Housing, Spatial Planning and the Environment)
VUT	Victoria University of Technology
WCED	World Commission on Environment and Development
WRF	World Resource Foundation
WRI	World Resources Institute